THEOLO
IN AN
INSURGENT
KEY

T0102185

Violence, Women, Salvation

Nancy Pineda-Madrid

2019 Madeleva Lecture in Spirituality

Paulist Press
New York / Mahwah, NJ

Cover and book design by Lynn Else

Library of Congress Cataloging-in-Publication Data
Names: Pineda-Madrid, Nancy, author.
Title: Theologizing in an insurgent key : violence, women, salvation / Nancy Pineda-Madrid.
Description: New York / Mahwah : Paulist Press, [2022] | Series: Madeleva lecture in spirituality | Summary: "What the author argues in this work is that violence against women today requires a rethinking of salvation. Yet, to make this case necessitates an understanding of violence against women in its particularity without which the author's argument, at best, will only limp along, falling flat, or remain an exercise in abstraction"—Provided by publisher.
Identifiers: LCCN 2021042819 (print) | LCCN 2021042820 (ebook) | ISBN 9780809155231 (paperback) | ISBN 9781587689185 (ebook)
Subjects: LCSH: Salvation--Catholic Church. | Women in the Catholic Church. | Catholic Church—Doctrines. | Women—Crimes against. | Women—Crimes against—Religious aspects—Christianity. | Violence—Religious aspects—Christianity.
Classification: LCC BT755 .P54 2022 (print) | LCC BT755 (ebook) | DDC 234—dc23
LC record available at https://lccn.loc.gov/2021042819
LC ebook record available at https://lccn.loc.gov/2021042820

ISBN 978-0-8091-5523-1 (paperback)
ISBN 978-1-58768-918-5 (e-book)

Published by Paulist Press
997 Macarthur Boulevard
Mahwah, New Jersey 07430
www.paulistpress.com

Printed and bound in the
United States of America

CONTENTS

INTRODUCTION

Ever since my first visit to Mexico City as an eleven-year-old child, I have always found myself swept up in the city's pulse and drama of life writ large, particularly when in the midst of the throngs of fascinating people crowding its grand avenues. This is nowhere more so than along Avenida de los Insurgentes, the longest avenue in Mexico City, which runs north-south and spans more than twenty-eight kilometers (over seventeen miles). This impressive avenue connects some of the city's most impoverished neighborhoods to some of its most exclusive and wealthiest ones. Mexico's early nineteenth-century upstart visionaries originally named this avenue for the army that fought for Mexican independence from Spain beginning in 1810, yet today this avenue is more commonly associated with the leaders of the Mexican revolution who fought in the early twentieth century. It is the long, consequential road taken by insurgents that stirs my imagination.[1]

An insurgent is one who rises up, who surges, who revolts against authority or established leadership, typically acting contrary to the policies and decisions of one's own government. An insurgent is one who is engaged in a kind of power play through a political movement or force that *gradually* infiltrates and subverts the reigning paradigms of thought and behavior. An insurgent moves in ways far more subtle and gradual than an insurrectionist, even though both are out to challenge long-standing ways of thinking and leading. An insurgency, the work of many insurgents, may go on mostly unnoticed for an extended period of time before its transformational impact becomes all too evident.

While *insurgency* is a term of art common in the political realm, might it also be imperative in the theological realm? Does the horror of today's inescapable and escalating violence against *women as women* (especially brown and black women) require of us an insurgent theology? One that rises up against the pervasive, corrosive, and destructive impact of a societal order that obliviously breeds evil? What role has theology played and what role does theology continue to play in the ongoing violence against *women as women*?

Violence against *women as women* here refers to gender-based violence against women of color, meaning violence deeply rooted in a system of structured gender and racial inequalities that overwhelmingly targets women (and children and some men). It is violence motivated by a drive to assert and maintain structural gender and racial inequalities. In an effort to maintain these inequalities, this violence employs

glossed-over misogynistic and racial ideologies as jus-
tifying tropes. This is a violence born of many factors,
not least of which is a social, cultural ethos that too
often fails to question why violence is widely perceived to be part of masculinity.[2] Where does Christian theology locate itself in the face of this deadly
scourge?[3]

Without question, every century for millennia and
every continent around the world has its own terrifying stories of violence against women. Still, in our own
time, and again on virtually every continent, the systematic killing of women because they are women has
escalated significantly. For more than two decades,
this extreme form of violence, known as feminicide,
has increased in North America and Europe as well as
in Asia, Africa, and the Middle East, as documented
by reports from the UN and from the World Health
Organization.[4] Yet, this tragedy is most acute in Latin
America, particularly in Mexico, Brazil, Guatemala, El
Salvador, Honduras, Bolivia, Argentina, Peru, Venezu-
ela, Colombia, and Paraguay, among other countries.
Feminicide, the assassination of women because they
are women, is distinguished by three characteristics:
(1) a large number of assassinations of women by
men;[5] (2) the brutal, sexual nature of these assassinations; and (3) a system of impunity for the perpetrators, as I have discussed at length elsewhere.[6]

This violence is part and parcel of a gruesome,
macabre paradox. At the same time that women in
large numbers around the globe have stepped into

significant positions of public leadership—as members of Congress, university professors, doctors, lawyers, pastors, recognized leaders of business and industry—women are also being brutally assassinated in ever-increasing numbers around the globe. No longer an epidemic, extreme violence against women has become a pandemic. Violence against women has marked the human situation for millennia, yet our own time has seen not only a greater consciousness of the widespread systematic killing of women because they are women, but also a greater willingness to mobilize against such violence and demand that it end. This widespread systematic killing of women issues a soteriological imperative. If Catholic theology is to remain true to the gospel's promise that "all flesh shall see the salvation of God" (Luke 3:6), including women's flesh, then Catholic theology must reimagine salvation. Women's lives and bodies must be located explicitly and unequivocally within the salvation imaginary of Catholic theology.

Everything is at stake. Women's bodies have been disappeared, literally, to be sure, but symbolically as well. Where do we locate women's bodies in theology? This book interrogates the question of salvation as it erupts amid violence against women as women, recognizing this violence's global scope and the dynamic nature of its destructive impact. To what degree do brown and black women's lives matter? As much as white men's? If Catholic theology is to affirm the supreme value of brown and black women's lives, and

4

to do so both symbolically and literally, then it cannot but reimagine salvation by locating brown and black women's bodies at the center of its understanding of salvation. The phenomenon of feminicide—the most extreme affront to the value of women's lives, one of the most heinous evils in the world today—requires just such prophetic work if Catholic theology is to be a force for good and not a discourse that turns a blind, passive eye to evil. Short of this kind of rethinking, Catholic theology undermines its summons to belief in the God who saves. The time is now. Women's lives are at stake. If we do not recognize feminicide as a contemporary crucifixion, and if we do not recognize our need for a message and vision that impels us to see vividly that all human beings are essentially intercon-nected, then our belief in the God who saves is ren-dered limp and, in the end, irrelevant. This crucifixion of many women and girls reflects a grossly misformed social imagination. We need a gripping vision of Christ's salvific presence that denounces feminicide. We need an insurgent soteriology.

To begin, how does the question of salvation become an urgent, insistent concern? What in the human con-dition leads to the question of salvation? Why does this question become urgent and insistent, demanding a response? How does our inclination toward hope play a role? After having clarified the conditions and emergence of the question of salvation, this small book next asks what fuels violence against *women as women*? What is this kind of violence? This work focuses attention on the most extreme form of violence against women as women, that is, feminicide, identifying various examples that illustrate the distinctive character of feminicide. In a precipitous manner, it is escalating in various Latin American countries as well as around the globe. While the Ciudad Juárez feminicide has been the most widely studied, feminicides are also ongoing in Guatemala, Honduras, Peru, El Salvador, Colombia, and Argentina, among many other countries. Given these examples, how does violence against women as women particularize the eruption of the question of salvation? This book delineates why and how these assassinations require an insurgent theology. Third, if our understanding of salvation is to remain true and compelling, then it must locate the most vulnerable at the center. Indeed, it must foreground the victims and survivors of feminicide. What are the guiding assertions for an understanding of salvation in the shadow of feminicide? Finally, and most significantly, based on the guiding assertions, what might a credible and authentic Catholic understanding of salvation look like? What does it mean to affirm that all flesh shall see the salvation of God, especially the crucified people of today, women? Which norming theological narratives need to be troubled? Only by re-membering the crucified victims as part of Christ's body can we have credible hope in the possibility of salvation.

I

GIVING RISE TO THE QUESTION OF SALVATION

In general, what gives rise to the question of salvation? *Negative experiences*—sometimes called *negative contrast experiences*[1]—provoke a search for meaning and a desire for something more. Eventually all humans experience some form (or many forms) of suffering brought on by ignorance, sin, guilt, pain, and death, among other conditions. These negative experiences often give rise to feelings of confusion, disbelief, disillusionment, and despair. As a result, we may question the meaning of life, the intractable presence of evil, the seeming inability to choose regularly what is good, the diminishment of human capacities in the face of serious illness or old age, and, most of all, the finality of death. These negative experiences and limit situations, all integral to the human condition, generate a constant tension between the brute givenness of what is and "the elemental human desire to be."[2]

Negative experiences emerge out of our limited views, our finitude. The fragmentary and broken character of our lives comes about, in part, from the narrowness of our view of life. Not only are our lives marked by conflicting motives but also by a frustrating inability to bring into harmony the varied and competing interests in our lives. Frequently, our own actions merely perpetuate and exacerbate the disharmonies in our lives. Moreover, at any given moment in time we only have the capacity to focus on a very limited range of facts. Even for those of us with a greater capacity for this kind of focus, we still, nonetheless, experience real limits. This existential limitation in the human condition gives way to human sorrow in that as individuals we cannot transcend this limitation even as we recognize it and desire a wider span of consciousness.[3]

More often than not, the serious tragedies of life come about as a result of our own natural narrowness of outlook. This natural narrowness of view mars our individual lives as well as our collective or social lives. On a social level, this natural narrowness can and often does lead to social sin in the form, for example, of racism, sexism, and homophobia. As Josiah Royce cautions,

Salvation itself is at stake in this struggle for a wider clearness of outlook. The wisest souls...agree with common-sense prudence in the desire to see at any one instant greater varieties of ideas and of objects than our form of consciousness permits us to grasp. To escape from the limitation imposed upon us by the natural narrowness of our span of consciousness...is the common interest of science and of religion, of the more contemplative and of the more active aspect of our higher nature.[4]

However, only God, who is infinite, enjoys limitless consciousness. Our finitude, by contrast, is the condition for the possibility and likelihood of pernicious behavior with tragic consequences.

Negative experiences emerge out of our encounter with evil, the root of suffering. Arguably, nothing provokes terrifying uncertainty like the experience of evil. Evil confronts us and demands some reckoning of us, a precarious challenge for two fundamental reasons. First, evil resists complete comprehension. As Bernstein insists, "Interrogating evil falls in the space between two extremes. We cannot give up the desire to know, to understand, to comprehend the evil that we confront. If we did, we would never be able to decide how to respond to its manifestations. But we must avoid the extreme of deluding ourselves that total comprehension is possible."[5] Precarious because within the incomprehensibility of evil lies its allure. We stand transfixed in our disbelief, frozen, seemingly unable to respond. Second, as Hannah Arendt wisely recognized, evil is endlessly banal; in the end, it is not necessary for human beings to be motivated by evil in order to commit evil acts. Indeed, "Arendt's paradigmatic example is Eichmann, a bureaucrat who claimed in his trial that he was just following orders and whose primary motivation was to move up the hierarchy."[6] Advancing professionally, a rather ubiquitous desire often blindly pursued.

We learn something of how evil is produced by examining cultural representations, their narratives, and the messages they are made to carry. The power of captivating images and narratives resides in their ability to point us toward how we "ought to" think, all the while anesthetizing us to human pain and anguish. The horror of evil is cloaked so that the workings of evil remain normalized. In the process, we come to see evil as banal, extreme at times, unfortunate always, but ultimately unavoidable. If we take evil seriously, we come to recognize that evil, while extreme and horrifying, is never radical. As Arendt knowingly discerned,

> It is indeed my opinion now that evil is never "radical," that it is only extreme, and that it possesses neither depth nor any demonic dimension. It can overgrow and lay waste the whole world precisely because it spreads like a fungus on the surface. It is "thought-defying," as I said, because thought tries to reach some depth, to go to the roots, and the moment it concerns itself with evil, it is frustrated

because there is nothing. That is its "banality." Only the good has depth and can be radical.[7]

If we agree that evil is ultimately thought defying, then we need to come to terms with the potent cultural representations that keep evil rooted in place. This necessarily takes us to the realm of the social imaginary, the everyday ways in which ordinary "people imagine their social existence, how they fit together with others, how things go on between them and their fellows, the expectations that are normally met, and the deeper normative notions and images that underlie expectations."[8] This realm is rarely one articulated in theoretical terms but rather consists of commonly held expectations and practices that are tacitly perceived to be normal and so command a large measure of legitimacy. We must recognize and interrogate the operative workings of evil at this prethematic level if we are to undertake the subversion of evil, a task central to the work of salvation.[9]

Relatedly, while our human finitude (natural narrowness of outlook) does not determine our self-consciousness, it does exert a strong influence, so much so that we often misunderstand one another. Indeed, "the greatest evil of human social life lies not in the elemental greed, the selfishness of men, but in their failure to understand one another."[10] "Understand one another" refers to recognizing and cherishing the full humanity of the other as well as appreciating deeply the vicissitudes of their lives. Even though humans do not bear responsibility for their condition of finitude and the way that finitude inevitably limits their responses to another, humans do bear responsibility to deepen and expand what capacity they have to respond to others, in other words, compassion and empathy. Humans do bear responsibility for the use, or misuse, of this capacity over the course of their lifetimes. Eventually, as Shakespeare's King Lear learned, in life each of us finds ourself confronting terrifying uncertainty and realizing that, while life brings goodness, evil and death more often than not remain close at hand, so much so that it is difficult to tell which will triumph in the end. Our capacity and desire to understand one another, or the lack thereof, will either help us subvert evil or not.

The experience of evil provokes suffering, among other negative experiences, raising the urgent question: Where is relief to be found? How might we find relief from the disillusionment, despair, cynicism, confusion, hopelessness, unimaginable horror, the distortion of life's value wrought everywhere? The presence of evil creates a soul-numbing vertigo. Where might we turn for some relief, some way forward that is worthy of trust? Where is light to be found in a world burdened by the crushing weight of senseless suffering? How are we to understand the presence of evil and why it plagues the human condition? And, where and how to find relief?

Almost always we come to recognize *our need* for salvation, neither exclusively nor even primarily through our reception of an external revelation such as the Bible, but rather as a result of our individual experience of the fragmentary, broken, and capricious character of our lives. As individuals and as society, sooner or later in life, experiences arise that bear the potential to open up the depth dimension of life, the deep-seated yearning for greater meaning, for the more that life could be. Indeed, all such experiences are religious experiences.

More to the point, our consciousness of our need for salvation depends upon our recognition of two primary ideas, both of which stem from the question, what is worthy of my life, of my lifetime effort? "The first," urges Royce, "is the idea that there is some end or aim of human life which is more important than all other aims, so that, by comparison with this aim all else is secondary and subsidiary, and perhaps relatively unimportant, or even vain and empty." The second idea is that each human being, left to their own devices, is "in great danger of so missing this highest aim as to render [her or] his whole life a senseless failure by virtue of thus coming short of [her or] his true goal."[11] Note that this is not to suggest that there exists a singular blueprint for each human life that must be discovered and pursued, but rather that there is a purposeful orientation to life that may be realized through a wide number of endeavors. The purposeful orientation to life is living in service of the greater good. This is what matters. We come to clarity concerning these two primary ideas by means of several "religious insights."

Religious insight consists, first, of knowledge that calls our attention to the interrelated nature of the many elements of our lives, suggesting to us our need for greater wholeness and self-possession, our need for salvation. Second, religious insight consists of knowledge about the path toward our salvation.[12] Religious insight encourages us to seek something external to ourselves that enables us to move toward our ideal purpose, something that delivers us from our broken, fragmentary, suffering state of life. Many living have already discovered this.

Yet, unless we experience internally our lack of and longing for a greater wholeness, a self-possession, the question of salvation remains an empty and meaningless concern. Many individuals move through life without ever discovering, much less attempting to realize, a purposeful life. While we become conscious of our hunger for self-possession through our own individual experience, our hunger is satisfied only when we learn to embrace and appreciate the essential interrelated quest for salvation of all human beings. This presence, external to ourselves, that can be our deliverer must be in some sense not only a power greater than the world but also a power that is enmeshed with the nature of reality. Thus, to attain this purposeful life, we need some sort of communion with a real life infinitely richer than our own—a life that is guided by a perfect and unwavering vision, and that somehow conquers and annuls all fickleness, conflict, and estrangement. Such a life rightly seems to us to be superhuman in its breadth of view and in its spiritual power, if indeed there be such a life at all. If there is no such life, nonetheless we need it, and so need salvation. If salvation is possible, then there is in the universe some being that knows us, and that is the master of life.[13]

Obviously, the master of life is God. What is critical here is the journey by which we come to an awareness of our need for salvation, of our need for a purposeful life, our need for God. The purposeful life that we long for and seek is a human project, but it is also always more. It transcends the human realm. "Without the question of salvation, there would be no religion at all because salvation simply gives specific content to the religious question."[14]

Given that religion begins with the question of salvation, salvation necessarily bears a narrative structure. First comes an experience of negativity or evil, an experience that provokes our awareness of our need to be saved. This then leads to a number of questions: Human beings need to be saved *from what*? And saved *for what*? In other words, what is the saved state of human existence? How are human beings saved? If salvation is "the experience-acceptance of a releasement from the

15

bondage of guilt-sin, the bondage of radical transitoriness and death, the bondage of radical anxiety in all its forms,"[15] then, how are any of us human beings drawn into the story of our salvation?

The horrific violence of feminicide being perpetrated today is one of the most extreme examples of evil that the world has known, so much so that it commands a response from Catholic theology. Simply put, this violence presses the question, Where are women's bodies located in the Christian salvation imaginary? Are women's bodies rendered invisible or secondary in the salvation imaginary? If "all human contact with God is historically mediated, that is, through finite things of this world,"[16] then how is the saving presence of God being mediated today as a blunt NO to the systematic violence and assassination that women are experiencing today because they are women?

What I am arguing in this work is that violence against women today requires a rethinking of salvation. Yet, to make this case necessitates an understanding of violence against women in its particularity, without which my argument, at best, will only limp along, fall flat, or remain an exercise in abstraction. The urgency of rethinking salvation *only* comes into view with an understanding of the particularities and specificities of violence against women to which this work now turns. The particularities shed light on and clarify why this project matters and is urgent.

II

VIOLENCE AGAINST WOMEN AS WOMEN

What is *violence*? The World Health Organization (WHO) defines it as "the intentional use of physical force or power, threatened or actual, against oneself, another person, or against a group or community, that either results in or has a high likelihood of resulting in injury, death, psychological harm, maldevelopment, or deprivation."[1] This definition amplifies a number of elements central to the following discussion of violence against women. First, violence entails the use of physical force to cause injury, damage, or death. Next, the harm intended (and caused) may extend well beyond the physical to include emotional, social, moral, spiritual, and psychic damage. Finally, the target of violence may be ultimately a group or community. In other words, violence can be symbolic in that the perpetrators inflict violence against a particular woman or group of women to send a message of threat to all women, reminding them that their own lives can meet a traumatic, brutal end. These three elements are all present in feminicide.

Due to its injurious intent, violence is immoral; it seeks to deny its human victims what is ethically owed to them. Violent injury to another person destroys their sense of self, their well-being, (at times) their freedom, and, in the case of feminicide, their lives. That said, an injurious intent may not be clear; reason does not always precipitate violence. Being radically contingent, violence can be triggered by an impetuous emotion and nothing more.[2]

As aforementioned, violence against women finds expression in a wide variety of forms, the most extreme being feminicide, the assassination of women because they are women. By any measure, feminicide is a *crime against humanity*. According to the United Nations, a "crime against humanity" refers to acts such as "murder," "extermination," "torture," "rape, sexual slavery, enforced prostitution," "any other form of sexual violence of comparable gravity," and "enforced disappearance of persons," among many other acts. A crime against humanity occurs when the acts are "committed as part of a widespread or systematic attack directed against any civilian population...pursuant to or in furtherance of a State or organizational policy to commit such attack."[3] Feminicide refers to male perpetrators engaged in a widespread, systematic attack against women that almost always includes sexual violence and ends with the brutal killing of women.

Further, in this work the term *feminicide* (or *feminicidio*) refers to the following: (1) women (and girls) are killed in large numbers; (2) these killings are brutal in nature and display signs of sexual violence; and (3) the state involved is culpable because it overlooks this crime, which, in effect, grants impunity to the perpetrators. Some scholars, informed by the work of anthropologist Marcela Lagarde, identify feminicide as genocide against women.[4] When the character of a society deteriorates, resulting in the violation of women's health, well-being, and freedom, then these violations further "the assumption that women are usable, abusable, dispensable, and disposable,"[5] and, over time, this contributes to a climate in which feminicide can erupt and develop. Today, nothing confronts belief in a good and loving God more sharply than the escalating crime of feminicide. Much earlier and relatedly, feminist theologian Mary Daly distinguished and named the brutal, systematic killing of women as women with her term *gynocide*.[6]

The phrase *women as women* recognizes that the violence discussed here must *not* be understood as simply one human being, who happens to be male, killing another, who happens to be female. Rather, *women as women* signifies the existential threat to all women in the violence of feminicide (among other forms of violence). This threat is advanced in an effort to extinguish in all women any aspiration of realizing their full humanity. To be sure, brown and black women are disproportionately far more vulnerable to the threat of lethal violence than are white women. I have made this argument elsewhere using what I call a *social suffering hermeneutic*.[7] How we see and regard the suffering of others matters greatly, especially that of feminicide victims and their surviving family members. All women confront an existential threat that is symbolized most horrifically in the assassinations of some women. Any would-be prophetic women who are in a situation of vulnerability are thus warned to keep silent, invisible, and mindful of their place. While feminicide issues a threat in its most extreme form, other related threats are also commonplace. Inhumanly and cruelly, we live in a time when political leaders have created a safe public space for misogynistic rhetoric (e.g., Brett Kavanaugh, Donald Trump, Jair Bolsonaro, Ted Yoho, among many others). Often, the threat comes because women refuse to play the role of sycophant pawns to men who wield corporate, political, or social power, deciding who is hired, promoted, or fired. Thankfully, we live in a time of courageous women— such as Christine Blasey Ford, E. Jean Carroll, Alexandria Ocasio-Cortez, and many others—who are unwilling to keep their mouths shut in the face of injustice.

Women as women signals that women today not only contend with a system of gender inequalities, but also, and more dreadfully, women invariably find themselves living within a *culture* of violence against women. As Susan Brooks Thistlethwaite contends, the cultural climate that foments violence against women becomes visible only when we stay focused on the physical pain inflicted on women's bodies. We need to stay at the physical level. This keeps us honest. "Staying with the body and what happens to the body begins to expose the gaping wounds caused by violence. The wounding of bodies, sometimes even unto death, poses an existential claim that is less easily dismissed than statistics, though the drive to dismiss, deny, minimize, or even authorize these wounds is strong."[8] Obviously, physical violence is not the only violence women know. Even so, the identification of this tolerated cultural violence gives rise to comments such as "not all men," comments that occlude our ability to see the culture of violence directed at women by shifting our attention to the behaviors of a few specific men. Thus, we end up cognizant of a number of individual men who behave horrifically, and in the process, we are unaware of a deeply disturbing cultural phenomenon.

Without a doubt, extreme violence against women has an ominous and millennia-long history. One widely cited example from the Christian biblical tradition is the heinous violence committed against the unnamed woman of Judges 19:1–30. She was brutally and repeatedly raped by a gang of men through the night; her bloodied and beaten body lay on a threshold of the home of an acquaintance. Later, with his knife, her "husband" cut her brutalized body into twelve pieces. He sent a piece of her body to each of the twelve tribes of Israel. Of course, tragically there are many more examples in the Scriptures and throughout history. In the early modern period, many thousands of women in several European countries were accused of witch-craft and executed, the common rationale being that women became witches because women were spiri-tually and morally weaker than men.[9] The practice of female infanticide has a long and documented history, notably in India and China as well as other countries. Dowry killings and honor killings likewise have a long history that stretches into our own time. The contem-porary phenomenon of feminicide, to which I now turn, is yet one more example of the long-standing traumatic and traumatizing extreme violence against women.[10]

Today, feminicide is a global problem. Feminicide is a polycentric eruption on virtually every continent of the world. It erupts—that is, it has and continues to break out in many communities, neighborhoods, cities, and countries around the world. Since the last decade of the twentieth century, feminicide has esca-lated rapidly, with notable eruptions in Asia, Africa, Australia, Europe, and North and South America. Matthias Nowak, on behalf of the Graduate Institute of International and Development Studies in Geneva, Switzerland, notes that across the globe there were about 66,000 victims of feminicide per year every year from 2004 to 2009.[11] More recently, The Global Americans reported that between 2007 and 2012, on average at least 60,000 women annually were killed violently.[12] To this day, the tragedy of feminicide continues. Globally, of the twenty-five countries with the highest rates of feminicide, fourteen are in the Americas. In 2018, the United Nations' Gender Equality Observatory reported that in absolute numbers Brazil and Mexico had the highest number of feminicide victims. Horrifically, though, the 2018 highest rates of feminicide per 100,000 women belongs to El Salvador (6.8), Honduras (5.1), Bolivia (2.3), Guatemala (2.0), and the Dominican Republic (1.9).[13] "In Guatemala two women are murdered on average each day; in Honduras feminicide is considered the second highest cause of death of women of reproductive age; in Bangladesh, in the first half of 2009, 119 cases of dowry-related violence including 78 deaths were reported; and in India there were an average of 8,000 reported cases of dowry death each year for the period 2007 to 2009."[14]

Feminicide demands the decisive attention of Christian theology in general and Catholic theology in particular. Evil of this nature and on this scale requires nothing less. Of the countries in the world with the largest absolute numbers of Catholics, Brazil is first and Mexico is second. Horrifically, both of these countries suffer from an extremely serious feminicide scourge. I am not suggesting any kind of direct or causal relationship with regard to this disturbing coincidence, but even so, Catholic theology must not turn a blind eye to the crucial role it can play by directly confronting the horrific evil of feminicide, thereby recognizing the theological significance of this scourge. The few statistics mentioned above paint a disturbing yet abstract impression of feminicide. Such is insufficient and ineffective to the goal of confronting the reality of this evil.

If Catholic theology is to play a role in deepening and expanding the faithful's capacity to follow Jesus, then it must "confront the concrete history in which we live, with all its complexity," as Jon Sobrino has argued.[15]

> Intellectually, this means grasping the truth of concrete reality; practically, it means responding to the demand made by that reality. More precisely, it means—and this is why this honesty is not so very much in evidence—coming to a grasp of truth and actually making a response to reality. This is accomplished not only by way of overcoming ignorance and indifference, but in confrontation with our innate tendency to subordinate truth and to evade reality.[16]

Ironically, just such a tendency is readily seen in the work of Catholic theologians who strongly profess an option for the poor yet fail to grasp the full truth of concrete reality when they turn a blind eye to the significance of gender.[17] To grasp the truth of concrete reality requires that we confront the material condition of women's bodies. Today's scale of worldwide eruptions of feminicide demands no less. What follows is an initial step toward confronting reality through a series of brief descriptions of feminicide in nine Latin American countries, chosen primarily because of the severity and seriousness of this evil there.

Such descriptions are necessary because many who first learn of feminicide do not believe that it could possibly be real, or, at most, they imagine that it is a localized tragedy in a few discrete locations. Both are erroneous.

Indeed, it is wise to be mindful of the ways in which accounts of extreme evil tempt and derail us. The spectacle of evil can hold us transfixed, so much so that we lose ourselves. The horror itself captivates because this evil is beyond our imagination, and yet, we find ourselves driven to understand what, at some level, cannot be fully understood. Then again, precisely because this evil persists on the far side of our imagination, we dismiss it as so inconceivable that it must be a fiction. The extreme horror of it makes us doubt its veracity. And still again, the preponderance and severity of evil can overwhelm us to such a degree that any desire or inclination we have to respond is crushed. We turn away exhausted by the very idea of taking responsibility for the real. The enormity of it all is too much to bear. Recognizing these temptations, we are called, nonetheless, to confront the real.

Latin America, with the highest rate of feminicides in the world,[18] offers a consequential depiction of this global problem. Below, the terms *feminicide* and *femicide* are used somewhat interchangeably. Scholars today have yet to achieve a widely accepted consensus regarding the distinctive meaning of each term. In the descriptions below, I defer to the form used in the sources I consult. For my part, I prefer *feminicide* because scholars use it more consistently to signify large numbers of victims and a pattern of impunity for the perpetrators.[19] Sometimes, *femicide* is used to imply these characteristics but certainly not always.

Mexico: Since the mid-1990s, the Ciudad Juárez, Chihuahua, feminicide has been among the most widely documented and studied.[20] It began in 1993, shortly after the passage of the North American Free Trade Agreement (NAFTA). Due to NAFTA, the Mexico–U.S. border became much more porous, allowing goods manufactured in Mexico to cross the border easily into the United States. Numerous U.S. corporations built manufacturing plants in Mexico along the south side of the border so as to take advantage of lower labor costs, far less powerful labor unions, and less restrictive laws protecting worker's rights and the environment. While the newly porous border greatly benefitted U.S. corporate interests, at the same time it drew the significant attention of drug cartels as an advantageous location from which to supply the United States's demand for illegal drugs. Rather quickly, substantial drug cartel operations moved into Ciudad Juárez and transformed the city's culture into one marked by the highest levels of crime and corruption, a level unsurpassed in Ciudad Juárez's long history. The ensuing climate of lawlessness, violence, terror, and an unparalleled influx of money together created a context ripe for the eruption of feminicide.

By the late 1990s, journalists and scholars began detecting a pattern in the assassinations of women and girls in various locations throughout the city. Female victims were typically between the ages of ten and twenty-nine. Their perpetrators most often raped, beat, and then brutally murdered them. Many had their breasts and vaginas savagely cut up before they were killed. It is nearly impossible to obtain an accurate count of the number of victims of this feminicide. There are, of course, different variables that distinguish this kind of violence. Sociologist and leading authority Julia E. Monárrez Fregoso, in her well-researched and meticulous study, reported that perpetrators assassinated 382 girls and women between 1993 and 2004.[21] Yet, she and others readily acknowledge that the number of victims is much higher, probably in the thousands. *El Paso Times* journalist and feminicide investigator Diana Washington Valdez reported that as of April 2009 perpetrators had raped, tortured, and murdered more than 600 women and girls.[22] Since then, *Al Jazeera* journalist Chris Arsenault reported that 878 women and girls were killed in Ciudad Juárez between 1993 and early 2011.[23] A clear account of the numbers of victims is difficult to obtain. Perpetrators have threatened and, in many cases, killed journalists, scholars, and other investigators because perpetrators want to continue their reign of terror unimpeded. More recently, the bodies of women and girls have been disappeared, compounding the difficulty of obtaining a clear account of this tragedy and furthering a reign of terror.[24]

While Ciudad Juárez was the early prominent face of feminicide in Mexico, feminicide has exploded throughout the country, particularly in greater Mexico City as well as in the states of Veracruz, Chiapas, Chihuahua, Nuevo Leon, Oaxaca, Sinaloa, Sonora, and Tamaulipas. According to the Observatorio de Igualdad de Género de América Latina y el Caribe, in 2018 alone the absolute number of feminicides in Mexico was 898, which was second only to the absolute number in Brazil of 1,206.[25] For the year 2019, Mexican authorities recorded 1,010 murders due to feminicide, but journalists and scholars suggest that this number is a serious undercount. Moreover, "Ninety-three percent of crimes in Mexico went either unreported or uninvestigated in 2018, according to a survey by Mexico's statistics agency."[26] Thus, systemic impunity has had a destructive impact on the pursuit of justice for victims of feminicide as well as victims of other crimes.

Central America and the Caribbean: The countries of Central America each have their own horrific histories of feminicide. **Guatemala**'s story of feminicide sprang from its internal armed conflict dating from 1960 to 1996 and concluding with the Guatemala Peace Accords. During the decades of conflict, the Guatemalan military and the Patrullas de Autodefensa

Civil (Civil Defense Patrols) used sexual violence and genocide as weapons of war to viciously target the indigenous Mayan population. The military and the patrullas trained a generation of young men to use rape and sexual violence systematically as a military "weapon of war" in rural areas suspected of supporting the guerilla effort. They employed rape and sexual violence to demonstrate domination over adversaries, and because these acts were "weapons of war," perpetrators enjoyed full impunity. Ever since the so-called end of the conflict in 1996, feminicide in Guatemala has escalated sharply, resembling the pattern of violence against women practiced during the war. Unlike Guatemalan males who are killed violently, the majority of women's murdered bodies reveal that they were raped, sexually mutilated, and tortured. In some cases, women's murdered bodies have been displayed in public so as to terrorize and intimidate the population.[27] In Guatemala, in 2010, 685 women were murdered,[28] and in 2012, that figure rose to 731 women. This second figure reflects a femicide rate of 9.7 murders per 100,000 women, the third highest rate in the world. Even though, in 2009, Guatemala was among the first Latin American countries to "declare femicide a punishable crime," this made little difference, because in Guatemala this law is not enforced and so femicide continues at a high rate, with perpetrators continuing to take impunity for granted.[29]

In 2012, **El Salvador** had an even higher murder rate than Guatemala, with an average of 12 murders per 100,000 women, the highest rate in the world. The UN High Commission on Human Rights reported that 647 women were killed in 2011 in El Salvador, a country notably smaller in size than the state of Massachusetts. In San Salvador, "residents are so inured to death and destruction that a woman's body lying in the street may cause little or no reaction." As journalist Angelika Albaladejo reported in 2016, "Within the current security crisis, gang and security force violence has exacerbated a broader, long-standing acceptance of violence against women....Impunity reigns in nearly all cases of violence against women."[30] Gang violence contributes significantly to feminicide in El Salvador, where women are quite often regarded as pawns in the battle for territorial dominance between rival gangs. "Gangs rape and violently murder young girls, or claim them as 'novias de las pandillas'—'girlfriends' of the gangs. 'Women's bodies were treated like territory during the civil war and continue to be today by the gangs,' says Jeanette Urquilla, the director of the Organization of Salvadoran Women for Peace (ORMUSA)." In many gang-controlled neighborhoods, young girls expect that gang members will rape, abduct, and/or murder them. Urquilla emphasizes that "this has led some families to pressure young women to become pregnant with their boyfriends, rather than be claimed by a gang member."[31] A woman with a connection to one gang (such as a sister or girlfriend) or a woman who lives in a neighborhood controlled by a particular gang is often targeted and murdered by members of a rival gang who are attempting to exert and expand their dominance.[32] Feminicide in El Salvador is sharply increasing. The Organization of Salvadoran Women for Peace (ORMUSA) reported that 329 women were killed in 2012; 215 in 2013; 292 in 2014; and 475 in the first 10 months of 2015.[33]

In 2012, **Honduras** had an average of 7 murders per 100,000 women, the seventh highest rate in the world. "Less than 2% of these murdered women's cases were investigated."[34] More recently, in 2018, 5.1 women per 100,000 suffered femicide.[35] Between 2006 and 2016, more than 4,400 women were murdered in Honduras.[36] The misogynistic, sadistic, and sexual violence characteristics of feminicide are everywhere evident. In one example, "women's naked, tortured bodies were found with their legs open as a demonstration of male power; and two young women were found dead with a message to the former presidential candidate written on their bodies, warning him off his campaign against criminal gangs (known as maras or pandillas)."[37] In Honduras, for women of reproductive age, femicide is the second highest cause of death.[38] The recent steep rise of drug trafficking in the countries of Guatemala, El Salvador, and Honduras has brought on a tragic coincidence: "a strong rise in drug trafficking coincides with an equally strong rise in female killings. In Honduras, the number of women killed per man has grown from 1 woman per 10 men to 4 women per 10 men. These murders follow other types of violence against women, such as sexual savagery, torture and mutilation."[39]

In describing feminicide in Central America, I focused on Guatemala, El Salvador, and Honduras because over the last decade, these three countries, horrifically, have been unwittingly competing with one another for the most dangerous country in the world for women. As the overall violence in each of these countries has escalated, the violence against women has been, and still is, on a much sharper climb. "In 2004 in Guatemala, murders of women increased 141 per cent, as opposed to 68 per cent for men; in El Salvador in 2006 murders of women increased 111 per cent, compared to 40 per cent for men; and in Honduras in 2007 murders of women increased 166 per cent, compared to 40 per cent for men."[40] Yet these three countries do not tell the whole story of feminicide in Central America.

Nicaragua, Costa Rica, Panama, and Belize each have their own accounts of feminicidal horror as well. "By the end of 2012, there were 1,813 victims of femicide in Central America, an increase of more than 670 women from the previous year. The victims were tortured, strangled, shot, burned or mutilated."[41]

A number of countries in the **Caribbean** also have horrifically high rates of femicide. For example, in 2018 the femicide rate per 100,000 women was 1.9 in the Dominican Republic, the fifth highest rate among all Latin American and Caribbean countries. Yet this same year, Trinidad and Tobago had an even higher rate of 3.4. And in 2017 Saint Lucia had a rate of 4.4.[42]

South America: While no South American country is untouched by the scourge of feminicide, what follows is a brief description of this evil in five countries. **Colombia**, like other Latin American countries, has seen an escalation of feminicide. Echoing the accounts above, in Colombia perpetrators brutally kill women for the purpose of sustaining a system of gender inequalities, ensuring the subordination of all women and, in particular, establishing male authority over women's bodies. According to the Instituto Nacional de Medicina Legal y Ciencias Forenses (INMLCF), of the 960 women murdered in Colombia in 2018, 73 of these killings were a femicide, the killing of a woman because she is a woman. Between January 1 and March 4 of 2020, 44 women and girls were victims of femicide in Colombia. Among the victims, "one 14-year-old girl was stripped naked and impaled, one 16-year-old girl was beheaded by her boyfriend and the youngest victim was only four years old."[43] In the wake of these femicides, two phenomena deepen the horror, that is, the impunity granted to the perpetrators and the decision of so much of the press to minimize, or ignore, the mass killing of women.[44]

Peru's story of feminicide has some parallels to Guatemala but also notable contrasts. In both countries, armed conflict preceded the eruption of feminicide, and in both, the perpetrators of brutal violence targeted their large indigenous population. However, scholars' work on Guatemala's feminicide reveals a widely recognized explicit connection between the eruption of feminicide and the country's internal armed conflict. In contrast, in research on Peru, scholars did not find this same connection. Peru's 1980–2000 armed conflict involved three parties: (1) the Communist Party of Peru—Shining Path; (2) the Tupac Amaru Revolutionary movement; and (3) the national armed forces. For most of the first decade of the twenty-first century, scholars examined, on one hand, the sexual violence stemming from this armed conflict, and on the other hand, Peru's feminicide as two distinct unrelated instances of violence against women. In the aftermath of Peru's armed conflict, its Truth and Reconciliation Commission (TRC) identified the majority of the tens of thousands of victims, men and women, as Andean Quechua-speaking peoples. In the main, the TRC attributes this violence to racism and the long-standing historical oppression of indigenous peoples. Initially, the TRC did not conduct a gendered analysis of its findings. After some TRC employees pushed for a gendered analysis, TRC began to report that of all the acts of sexual violence in this conflict, 83.46 percent of them were executed against women.[45]

Another organization within Peru, Estudio por la Defensa de los Derechos de la Mujer (DEMUS),[46] focused its attention on Peru's feminicide. DEMUS critiqued those who reduce the meaning of feminicide to the assassination of women by their male partners, while ignoring the impact of political violence. Too often, according to María Ysabel Cedano, the director of DEMUS, this kind of analysis does not take into account the way patriarchy and eruption of social trauma are interrelated. As a result, the political dimension of feminicide gets occluded. In Peru, the term *feminicide* has been used most often to discuss the familial violence against women in a way that diverts attention away from the truism "the personal is political," and in a way that fails to recognize the wider social institutionalization of sexism, racism, ethnocentrism, and power. In Peru, *feminicide* carries a meaning distinct from how it is understood in Mexico or Guatemala. From a legal perspective, feminicide has been relegated to the private sphere, in keeping with the erroneous idea that male domination of women is a private matter.[47]

Among Latin American countries battling feminicide, **Brazil** is infamous for two reasons. First, in 2018, it had the highest number of feminicide victims in the world at 1,206, and second, also in 2018, *The Global Americans* reported that Brazil had the worst records documenting gender-based violence, records that lack quality data.[48] Moreover, in Brazil perpetrators often "justify" violence against dark-skinned women, especially black women, on the basis of race, class, and ethnicity. Black women suffer a greater vulnerability to feminicide at the hands of "nonblack, non-lower-class men."[49] Indeed, race figures prominently in determining which women are more likely to become victims. Yet, the Brazilian Senate and House of Representatives did pass landmark legislation against feminicide in March 2015. However, the implementation of such legislation remains spotty at best, not only in Brazil but also throughout Latin America.

In 2018, **Bolivia** had a rate of 2.3 femicide victims per 100,000 women, the highest rate of any South American country and the fifth highest rate among all Latin American and Caribbean countries.[50] And in February 2020, the Economic Commission for Latin America and the Caribbean (ECLAC) and the Gender Equality Observatory for Latin America and the Caribbean both confirmed that Bolivia remains the South American country with the highest rate of feminicide.[51]

Between 2008 and 2017, 2,679 women and girls were victims of feminicide in **Argentina**, according to the nation's Observatorio de Femicidios, which also reported that the first six months of 2018 saw 139 women and girls fall victim to femicide.[52] Femicide in Argentina has a history more than two decades long. Since 1996, a pattern of violence against women coupled with the disappearance of women became apparent in the Mar del Plata region. Before they became victims, the murdered women were typically forced, violently or economically, into prostitution. Indeed, prostitution networks, at the center of these crimes, trafficked women within Argentina and later brutally murdered them. The forced disappearance of women was able to continue because of the complicity of police, state and judicial authorities, and members of the Argentine army. Police in the Mar del Plata region often collected money from prostitution networks in exchange for police silence. The number of murdered and disappeared women remains unknown. In this region and elsewhere in Argentina, a system of impunity has allowed forced prostitution and the killing of women to thrive.[53] Argentine scholar Marta Fontenla has identified this pattern as femicide, a crime that has been allowed to thrive in an extensive climate of impunity for the perpetrators.

The aforementioned accounts are, tragically, only a handful of examples of what is a much more widespread evil erupting in every country in Latin America and the Caribbean, not to mention in many countries around the world. The specifics of this evil in particular Latin American countries are offered here to make credible the reality of this extreme evil. Like so many other evil atrocities committed by human beings, feminicide has been for too long dismissed as an abstraction or as a tragic but minor localized phenomenon rather than taken seriously as widespread phenomena that makes demands on all would-be disciples of Jesus Christ.

Again, feminicide is not exclusively a Latin American and Caribbean horror. The rate at which women are being murdered because they are women is high and climbing in **Eastern Europe** (e.g., Russia, Kazakhstan, Belarus, Latvia, Ukraine, Lithuania, Serbia, Bosnia-Herzegovina, Croatia); in **Africa** (e.g., South Africa, Congo, Rwanda); and in **Asia** (e.g., India, China, Pakistan, Hong Kong, Japan, South Korea, Thailand, Sri

Lanka, Afghanistan, the Philippines).[54] In the United States, there are examples of this kind of violence as well, almost always suffered by women of color, especially indigenous women.[55] This heinous evil is much more extensive than what has been briefly described here. As Thistlethwaite so insightfully protests, "[The War on Women] is global and there are signs it is accelerating as women's bodies pay the price for anxieties and dislocations created by globalization."[56] As an extreme example of the war on women, feminicide is the product of globalized neoliberal capitalism coupled with racism, patriarchy, and colonialism.

No doubt, feminicide is in every sense a heinous evil, one that strains the outer limits of credulity. How can this be? What could possibly give rise to this kind of evil? And, most notably, where to locate theology's response?

To be able to take hold of this last question—where to locate theology's response—requires an initial grasp of some of the underlying forces that have given rise to this evil.

Over time, Western culture has normalized violence against women by means of its enduring Greek myths, some of its most celebrated art, and many of its most popular films, to name a few. Indeed, we "learn," with overwhelming frequency, that the nature of heroism comes more clearly into view through acts of violence against women, as Thistlethwaite has warned. Within these narratives, depictions of rape, conquest, and gender violence shape our deep-seated social imaginary (our widely held but unthematized social expectations of one another) in a manner that does not shame the male perpetrator but, rather, increases his position of honor. For example, Greek mythology repeatedly identifies as female the monsters who prey on civilization and as invariably male the hero who eventually slays the monster. In fine art, such as the celebrated Italian Renaissance painting by Titian, *The Rape of Europa* (ca. 1560–62), the male conquest of the female is glorified. The aesthetic of this painting is so exquisite that it discourages any would-be critique of the rape being depicted. Eros "sanitizes" violence against women, making it more palatable, rendering it incidental. Popular films such as the *Passion of the Christ* mythologize Jesus as a handsome, white American man who eventually conquers the serpent Satan depicted in feminized terms.[57] In addition, particular biblical narratives bear out this same kind of dynamic wherein women function as pawns in the exchange between men, a means by which honor is extended from one man to another (such as in Gen 20:1–16; Judg 19:1–30; 11:29–40). Violence against women becomes the collateral damage in the exchange.

Over and over again, heroism is demonstrated through the conquest of the female. This kind of mindset and paradigm is able to endure in Western culture because "violence against women is eroticized." Thistlethwaite rightly contends,

> There is perhaps no better definition of patriarchy than this equation of the will with "male power" dominating nature conceived as female. Myths, art, and modern mythologists all co-conspire to keep the foundations of normalized violence against women strong. Patriarchal domination gets identified as "love" in the West over and over through repetition and display....Sexual violence is OK, apparently, as long as you include Cupid in the scene and the abduction and rape is reframed as love.[58]

Relatedly, ingrained kyriarchal patterns of thought pose an existential threat to the racialized bodies of poor women of color, making them the targets of violence. Kyriarchy, of course, includes patriarchy but is broader in scope. It

> seeks to express this interstructuring of domination and to replace the commonly used term patriarchy, which is often understood in terms of binary gender dualism....[Kyriarchy is used] to articulate a more comprehensive systematic analysis, to underscore the complex interstructuring of domination, and to locate sexism and misogyny in the political matrix or, better, patrix of a broader range of oppressions.[59]

The existential threat to poor women of color takes many forms, foremost a threat to their bodily existence. Given that bodily existence is the bedrock of being human, perpetrators of extreme violence, with their all but inevitable kyriarchal patterns of thought, will strongly tend to target and assassinate brown and black women (along with other women of color). Whenever Christian theology loses sight of this thought pattern, it becomes complicit in the phenomenon of "intimate and societal violence." As a result, "violence itself is lauded as a divinely authorized rule instead of being seen as the ultimate insult to God's work in creating human beings and the world."[60] Indeed, many theologians today have taken up the challenge of interrogating so-called redemptive violence (such as Rita Nakashima Brock, Rebecca Ann Parker, Walter Wink, Denny Weaver, Delores Williams, S. Mark Heim, Carlos Mendoza-Álvarez, and Bob Daly, SJ, among many others).

In addition to the normalization of violence against women and ingrained kyriarchal patterns of thought, unrestrained neoliberal capitalism is likewise among the underlying forces that have given rise to the evil of feminicide. Ours is a time of impending global collapse brought on by the endgame of neoliberal capitalism, a time that announces the reign of death-dealing power. Feminicide cannot be considered but from within this larger economic narrative. Indeed, the rise of a perverse necropower depicts human beings as disposable commodities with a limited shelf life to be determined by the almighty profit margin. Many of the brown and back women, victims of feminicide, have been presumed to carry greater economic value dead than alive. The death spiral of trafficking and feminicide in the Mar de Plata region of Argentina precisely exemplifies this horror. When trafficked women forced into prostitution no longer turn a sufficient number of lucrative tricks each night, they are systematically assassinated. The Ciudad Juárez feminicide offers yet another example. Since the mid-1960s, and sharply after the early 1990s, maquiladores employed women in large numbers, which, on the one hand, allowed them to enter into public spaces and become breadwinners. And, on the other hand, this contributed to a view of women as commodities, to be used, consumed, and discarded.[61] Women, through their wages, obtained purchasing power that enabled them to have greater economic independence. However, this change also led to attacks on women by some men who resented the growing subversion of their patriarchal power, and thus they killed women in an effort to reestablish control of women and their bodies.

Indeed, the kyriarchal interstructuring of domination (including white supremacy, patriarchy, and plutocracy) plays a significant role in "authorizing" violence against women as women, with patriarchy being dominant. For example, patriarchy informs the use of women's bodies as the physical territory upon which men compete with one another, each seeking to establish his dominance. "Gang rape exhibits this characteristic to a great degree, where men use violence on a woman's body to gain power and status with and over other men."[62] Rape and feminicide in El Salvador are an unmistakable and extreme example.

A patriarchal pattern of thinking has been, and remains, very much a part of the Christian tradition and the practice of faith among Catholics. This raises the question, Where is Catholic theology located amid the ways in which patriarchal patterns of thought contribute to authorizing violence against women? Responding to this question is complicated, fraught with challenges, necessitating a cautious approach. History offers many examples of accusations against religion as the cause of some tragic evil, and then this accusation is used to justify an aggressor country's violent military action with the sanitized "goal" of saving women in danger of violence when the real goal is to extend colonial or imperial power. Native American women and Mexican women were used in this manner to justify the nineteenth-century U.S. pursuit of land, wealth, and power. Further, as Janet Jakobsen contends,

> If we simply assert that religion is a problem, necessarily bad for women and a direct source of violence, we can provide aid and comfort to US imperialism and the violence that it entails. Simultaneously, we may paradoxically strengthen rather than weaken the claims of those who justify violence through

religious discourses, even as we also create diffi-
culties for alliances with religious feminists across
traditions. Religious feminists are put in a position
in which they look either inauthentically feminist
or inauthentically religious.[63]

Even so, we must recognize that

> there are social, cultural, and religious supports
> that a society needs to employ in order to ensure
> that more than a third of women in that society can
> be treated violently, or threatened with violence,
> without mass outcry and rebellion. These social,
> cultural, and religious supports overlap with many
> of those that are necessary for societies to be will-
> ing to send the young, healthy bodies of its citizens
> into war, where many of them will be maimed or
> killed, also without mass outcry or rebellion.[64]

Like the violence of war, violence against women is
everywhere, yet "strong social, cultural, religious, and
economic forces conspire to hide" this violence, making it even more crucial and urgent that Catholic theology give witness to violence against women.

Not only must we attend to the underlying forces
that have given rise to feminicide, but we must also
attend to what allows all violence against women as
women, including feminicide, to continue flourishing. Almost always, violence against women continues
unseen, seemingly invisible. Its invisibility underscores

the need for a laser focus on the well-being of women's bodies.

> The damage to the body is an undeniable fact of violence; so too are the threats of violence that are carried not only in the mind but also in physical changes due to stress. The fact of the physical effects of violence on women's bodies, however, is aggressively hidden, qualified, reframed, reorganized, catalogued, excused, and ultimately authorized. This is how such a monumental amount of carnage continues almost unabated with very little public outcry or sustained efforts to stop it.[65]

And when the violence is noted publicly, all too often culpability is directed at the perpetrators exclusively, which, in turn, occludes our ability to see the violence as a cultural phenomenon.

What is left unseen is that we live amid a culture that foments violence against women. The only way to see this is by remaining committed to seeing the physical pain inflicted on women's bodies. We need to stay at the physical level. This keeps us honest. Thistlethwaite challenges us: "Staying with the body and what happens to the body begins to expose the gaping wounds caused by violence. The wounding of bodies, sometimes even unto death, poses an existential claim that is less easily dismissed than statistics, though the drive to dismiss, deny, minimize, or even authorize these wounds is strong."[66] There is so little outcry to stop this violence because erotics has been used to normalize it. Erotics has been used to make this violence appear desirable and thus as serving the interests of the typically white political and economic elite.

Concurrently, a particular reading of religion is often deployed as a cultural mechanism to make violence appear palatable and unavoidable even if it is disturbing. Indeed, religion, understood as primarily a sacrificial system, can placate many varied experiences of dehumanization and domination. The symbolic narratives central to religious practice can be retold in a manner that makes space for "subordination, abnegation and death,"[67] such that it becomes next to impossible to honestly see violence against women for what it is.

To see honestly the violence of feminicide for what it is serves as the first step toward the subversion of this heinous evil. Undeniably, feminicide is a social sin. Social sin stems from a corruption of the social good, that is, a society built on fair and just relations among all of its members. Corruption takes root and grows when a multitude of intersecting individual decisions collectively lead to social oppression of people of color, of the economically poor, and of women. Corrupt individual decisions reflect a "massive and cumulative moral failure of human intelligence and human responsibility."[68] This widespread moral failure hardens into morally bankrupt social systems and thought patterns, all with a "logic" that crucifies people. These social systems and thought patterns render some bodies economically more valuable dead than alive, in a word, necropolitics.[69]

Social sin stems not only from a moral corruption of social structures, systems, and cultures, but also from an obstructed view of this moral corruption. It remains hidden within all kinds of bureaucratic structures and policies. As M. Shawn Copeland has warned us, "a society in which structural oppression holds sway equals a society structured by and in social sin."[70]

As many theologians have emphasized, the Christian theological tradition has left its imprint on violence against women by charging Eve (and, by association, women) as primarily responsible for the emergence of sin in the world.

> While Genesis origin stories imply this, it is the New Testament narratives where this particular theological connection is made as in "First Timothy 2:12–14" that reads, "I do not allow women to teach or to have authority over men. They must keep quiet. For Adam was created first and then Eve. And it was not Adam who was deceived. It was the woman who was deceived and broke God's law."[71]

This particular "theological" mindset tills the soil, making way for the seeds of misogyny that eventually erupt into violence against women and, in the extreme, feminicide.

Without a doubt, this death-dealing "theological" mindset must be disowned. It has further deepened women's unresolved hunger for a theological vision grounded in women's experience of being embodied. This hunger flatly insists upon a theological vision "developed outside the narrow confines of patriarchal ideology."[72] Short of an earnest theological commitment to the goodness of women's bodily selves, violence against women as women will not be called out unequivocally. If such violence is not called out, then this lapse leads to the assignment of women's bodies to the peripheries of theological consciousness, a ghostly concern bearing responsibility for sin but otherwise of little consequence. To say the least, such a lapse encourages a blindness to the social sin of feminicide.

On the other hand, any attempt to write theology from the bodies of the victims of feminicide produces a crisis. Why? Such an attempt foregrounds the mortal consequence of feminicide for poor women of color, and thus calls down "God's judgment upon the patriarchal ideologies, which have sadly pervaded Christian theology, a theology that silenced the multitudes."[73] Such an attempt stands in the tradition of liberation theologies of habeas corpus. It refuses to accept the disappearance of women's bodies. It insists upon their presence. Marcella Althaus-Reid has implored us to recognize their presence. This produces a crisis. Consider that social scientists such as Marcela Lagarde and Julia Monárrez Fragoso hold the state, in particular the judicial system, responsible for feminicide because these powers function in a manner that effectively grants impunity to perpetrators and renders women's security null.[74] Might Christian theology take a lesson? Do the church and Christian theology bear responsibility when it remains silent in the face of this atrocity, when it fails to speak out? And yet, to speak out brings women's bodies to the center of theological meaning-making within a Christian tradition that historically has been ill at ease, to say the least, with such a prospect. Anytime a spotlight shines on the patriarchal shortcomings of Christian theology, a crisis ensues.

This is not simply a crisis on a wide canvas that is Christian theology, but even more a crisis that holds open the possibility of agitating each of us deeply. The tragedy of feminicide requires of us, as disciples of Jesus Christ, to name feminicide in a manner such that we situate ourselves within its purview. To name it in this way inevitably affects the way we attempt to imagine and understand something of God. To write theology from the bodies of those victimized by feminicide recognizes that these women are daughters of the living God, and they remain present to us. This is unsettling. Ignacio Ellacuría once urged us to consider,

> Among so many signs always being given, some identified and others hardly perceptible, there is in every age one that is primary, in whose light we should discern and interpret all the rest. This perennial sign is the historically crucified people, who link their permanence to the ever distinct form of their crucifixion. This crucified people represents

the historical continuation of the servant of Yahweh, who is forever being stripped of his human features by the sin of the world, who is forever being despoiled of everything by the powerful of this world, who is forever being robbed of life, especially of life.[75]

How do we see reality as it comes at us in our own time? What sign is being given today? Our generation lives in a time of feminicide. What does it mean to believe in the God who saves when the "crucified people" of our time are the victims of feminicide?

More to my point, given the tragedy of feminicide, where do we locate women's bodies in soteriology? How do we speak of the God who saves in a time, paradoxically, when, on the one hand, increasing numbers of women have moved into positions of economic, social, political, intellectual, and cultural leadership, and, on the other hand, women as women are being brutally slaughtered and murdered in ever greater numbers and with impunity? If theology is to say no to the horror of feminicide and, thus, to support unequivocally the subversion of violence against women, then how we understand salvation presents a significant challenge. In the end, what is at stake is not women's will to power but rather the integrity of what salvation means. "If patriarchy is part of the structures of sin, as liberationists have argued, then theology needs to dismantle itself as well as announce a new way of doing theology. The presence of women's bodies in theology not only grounds but questions traditional theological reflection on redemption, sin, and grace."[76] Nothing puts this challenge before us more abruptly and urgently than feminicide.

III

SALVATION
IN THE
SHADOW OF
FEMINICIDE

In an age of feminicide, what does it mean to believe in the God who saves? How can such a belief have integrity and credibility? Might we, disciples of Jesus Christ, consider that our time is one of theological reckoning, that ours is a time of theological inflection? Might the eruption of feminicide around the globe be issuing a theological wake-up call? To what degree do we value, affirm, and act upon a theological vision that fiercely and unequivocally subverts the normalcy of violence against women as women?

Any credible theological response to these questions must first recognize feminicide as yet another iteration of the problem of evil. Accordingly, how are we to step into the fray of the stark contrast between what God wills for women and the brute givenness of feminicide? What does this contrast mean for our belief in the God who saves? Indeed, we must hear women's voices crying out, voices hungry for life. This hunger for life finds satisfaction only when we lean into the offer of the Giver of Life, the Holy Spirit, who beckons us to recognize, embrace, and appreciate the essential interrelated quest for the salvation of *all* human beings, indeed, of all creation. If we fail to hear the cries of those victimized by feminicide, those dead and alive, then we place our own salvation in jeopardy. Salvation is always social as well as personal. This recognition is salvation's imperative.

This line of theological questioning situates this book in the field of public theology and political theology—public theology in the sense that its primary concern is not with individual subjectivity, nor with clarifying church doctrines, but because its primary concern is the welfare of society. "Public theology," according to Duncan Forrester, "often takes 'the world's agenda,' or parts of it, as its own agenda, and seeks to offer distinctive and constructive insights from the treasury of faith to help in the building of a decent society, the restraint of evil, the curbing of violence, nation-building, and reconciliation in the public arena."[1] It is a work in political theology in the sense that it recognizes the ways in which theological discourse has an impact on and influences materially

54

the political and economic structures of society. Theology reflects, and serves to reinforce, what are either just or unjust political arrangements. Thus, this theological project understands the ways theological discourse can replicate many social inequalities of race, class, and gender to destructive effect. Such makes clear the need for a soteriological vision that affirms the God-given value of poor brown women who are most at risk of being brutally killed. The rising tide of feminicide demands no less.

As noted previously, through and because of human experiences of suffering, death, oppression, illness, ignorance, sin, brokenness, despair, loss, disorientation, fragmentariness, pain, evil—all negative contrast experiences (Schillebeeckx)—humans yearn for a release from their suffering, for greater healing, for wholeness, for liberation from oppression, and so forth. Indeed, Christians identify this yearning as the search for salvation. Christianity began because Jesus's first disciples experienced God's gift of salvation through their relationship with Jesus; they experienced "Jesus as a bringer of God's salvation." Christianity endures to this day because throughout its two-thousand-year history, disciples have continued to experience this same gift of salvation. For many theologians, myself included, "every Christian understanding of Jesus Christ has its source in the experience of salvation." This claim "finds expression in extensive historical and constructive reflection on the meaning of salvation."[2] If we human beings are unaware of *our need* to be saved, then the cogency of belief in an incarnate God who saves will fall on deaf ears. Our need to be saved can remain a claim met with minimal interest or even indifference; indeed, much today numbs our consciousness of our need or distracts us away from our suffering and pain, rendering limp our awareness of our need.

The remainder of this book attempts an initial understanding of the nature of Christian salvation that is credible in the shadow of feminicide. To begin, every Christian understanding of "salvation has both an objective and a subjective dimension and sense." The *objective* dimension is what Jesus Christ did for human beings that has a salvific effect on human existence. In other words, what is the salvation that is mediated through Jesus Christ? A full understanding of salvation must also include the *subjective* dimension, that is, "the appropriation of this salvific effect by human beings."[3] To consider salvation in the shadow of feminicide requires particular attention to the ways the survivors of feminicide (family members of the victims) have responded to God's saving presence mediated by Jesus Christ through the power of the Holy Spirit in the here and now. Given that feminicide is a social evil and a social sin, what is required is an understanding of salvation unequivocally attentive to the social character of salvation. Human beings' appropriation of salvation must not be reduced to isolated individual human actions alone but must take into account collective, social actions and evolving social structures and systems, which are also part of the subjective dimension of salvation.

Salvation's objective and subjective dimensions mean that salvation has a narrative structure. Humans experience a transformation *from* a negative situation *to* a better situation that is in some way freer, less broken, more liberated—in other words, the in-breaking of salvation into our present. Gustavo Gutiérrez has called this transformed situation one that reflects a growth of the kingdom of God.[4] The narrative structure comes into sharper focus when we come to understand more deeply not only what Jesus Christ did and does that bears a salvific effect for human beings (objective), but also how we human beings appropriate this salvific effect (subjective).

Even though salvation is of unparalleled importance to the Catholic Church and its theology, the church has never officially adopted a single formulation of the doctrine of salvation. Of course, there are primary commitments that distinguish a Catholic understanding of salvation: principally, that Jesus the Christ is the mediator of salvation, and that all human beings need salvation, claims without which we would not be speaking of a Christian understanding of salvation. Still, the Christian tradition across its two-thousand-year history has been receptive to pluralism in its understanding of salvation, recognizing the wide range of "human existential reality."[5] Such invites the endeavor to seek out a credible understanding of salvation in the shadow of feminicide.

Moreover, my pursuit of a credible understanding of salvation begins with a foundation of five guiding assertions that clear a space for the particular understanding of Christian salvation that then follows. The work of both Roger Haight, SJ, and Josiah Royce significantly inform my thinking in all that follows.

The *first* guiding assertion is that God reveals Godself in human history, in liberating historical events. Accordingly, salvation is rightly understood as something we experience, at least in part, in the here and now, in history, rather than exclusively in the afterlife. The in-breaking of the kingdom of God[6] in history, the intensification of God's grace in human history is the work of salvation. Consequentially, salvation is, to some degree, realized in history. Even so, this realization is not the whole of salvation, which only comes in the fullness of time, in eternity. As the unique and whole revelation of God, Jesus actively worked to realize the kingdom of God in history, ongoing work that the Holy Spirit continues into our own time and beyond. The ongoing saving work of Jesus is always in history.[7]

The in-breaking of the kingdom of God in history is the work of salvation, yet this in-breaking never occurs in the midst of a benign reality. Rather, it always takes place in the midst of the anti-kingdom, that is, the coalescence of various death-dealing forces that vitiate what God has created. Work on behalf of the kingdom of God always "brings out the reality of the historical anti-Kingdom."[8] Indeed, the coming of the kingdom of God, as Sobrino exhorts, necessitates a struggle against and "a triumph over the anti-Kingdom."[9]

The historical endeavor to subvert the evil of feminicide is work on behalf of the kingdom of God and is work of great complexity. The victims of feminicide must remain a dangerous memory for all disciples of Christ, haunting us so that we forge a world where feminicide is no more. "It is not those innocent of evil who are fullest of the life of God, but those who in their own case have experienced the triumph over evil."[10] Indeed, salvation can only be realized in a world in which it is in question. Thus, while we can never entirely rid the world of evil, we can subordinate and subvert it. We partially realize salvation in history when we seek the greatest good through the subordination of evil, which entails a critique of and a dismantling of death-dealing ideologies. However, when we experience evil, that is, when we suffer, particularly when we suffer unjustly, our initial inclination tends to be to destroy the source of our suffering, which is often another human being. Most often good and evil are bound up together such that the destruction of evil would destroy good as well. The human who responds by destroying does not realize the greater good, while the human who, having suffered, uses her or his suffering creatively toward some greater purpose allows all to glimpse a vision of the spiritual ascendancy of the good in history.[11] How we come to terms with what we have already suffered (past tense) is as crucial as our efforts to subvert the ills we can foresee.

The *second* guiding assertion affirms salvation as God's revelation. Salvation entails "a reconciliation between God and human existence"[12] that comes about through God's incessant, loving presence in our midst. Through God's self-communication with us, God constantly seeks the renewal and deepening of union with human beings: this is salvation. Jesus uniquely and fully reveals God's constant presence and ardent desire for communion with human beings and with all of creation. Yet there is more. Jesus's lifelong practice of loving us continuously actualizes our communion with God, making this communion ever more visible and relevant.

Salvation as revelation includes the whole of creation. Augustine and Aquinas, among many other theologians, have recognized that the whole of the natural world is revelatory of God, that it is the second book of revelation.[13] As Elizabeth Johnson has taught us, creation has three dimensions: (1) *creatio originalis* (the original gift of life given by God to plants and animals); (2) *creatio continua* (God's sustaining presence to plants and animals without which they would cease to exist); (3) *creatio nova* (God draws and renews all of creation by opening up new possibilities for the future).[14] These three dimensions of creation show us something of God's benevolence, capaciousness, and gratuitousness; and these dimensions beckon us into a deeper relationship with God, with one another, and with the whole of creation. This movement is salvific.

What is being revealed by God is the fundamental spiritual unity of the world. God's Spirit continuously draws and lures us all into communion with God, with all humanity, and with all that is in and of the world, indeed, every being in creation. It is supercommunion writ large. Evil utterly obscures this communion, attempts to destroy any sense of communion, and diverts human attention away from God's revelation. Accordingly, salvation in the shadow of feminicide must account for the most extreme, utter affront to the fundamental spiritual unity and communion that God wills for the world.[15]

The *third* guiding assertion is that salvation is nonsensical when it is *exclusively* reduced to a personal, individual concern. When understood as narrowly a personal, individual concern, our understanding of "salvation" slips into a kind of theological solipsism. This line of thinking implies a god who is uninterested in the human community as such and is only interested in individual lives. Certainly, this is not the God of Jesus Christ, not the God of Pentecost, not the God of the New Testament, and not the God of the Jews in the Hebrew Scriptures (Old Testament). While always personal and individual, salvation inevitably concerns the social givenness of human existence and beyond. Moreover, salvation as a personal, individual concern is nonsensical because, as Haight points out,

Human existence is a social phenomenon, so that even the individual, in his or her quasi-autonomy, is at the same time a function of social relationships, not to mention intrinsic, organic relationships with the world of nature. This anthropology of human solidarity describes an ontological condition; these relationships constitute persons whether or not they are always explicitly aware of their formational character.[16]

And, because "human existence is a social phenomenon," a social metaphysics can ground and contribute to a cogent Christian understanding of salvation. A social metaphysics is a way of understanding reality that takes our interrelatedness with all other human beings, all other creatures, and all that has being as fundamental to our self-understanding. If we hold that the nature, constitution, and structure of reality is fundamentally social, then we must recognize that this line of reasoning bears theological and soteriological significance, not only for the human community but also beyond as well.

Further, a social metaphysics implies a consciousness. Individual human consciousness and a social consciousness have meaning and value only in light of a larger unity of consciousness. "The whole reality of the universe itself must be defined in terms of the reality of such an inclusive and direct grasp of the whole sense of things."[17] All of humanity, nature, and creation is to be included in the grasp of the whole.

This larger unity of consciousness is a transcendent consciousness, a superhuman consciousness. This transcendent consciousness that constantly interrelates all that has being may be called the Interpreter Spirit, the immanent divine active in the world, God.[18]

To understand Christian salvation in the shadow of feminicide requires foregrounding of the human capacity to actively recognize the social constitution of human existence and actively participate in the transformation of the underlying social structures that fuel the possibility of feminicide and that are heinously sinful. If human beings remain passive or blind to the social structures and mechanisms that shape our lives, then religious discourse about salvation will appear unintelligible if not irrelevant.[19]

The *fourth* guiding assertion is that salvation is *integral* in nature, meaning that it takes into account the whole of life, every dimension of life without exception. "Salvation is an all-encompassing concept that reaches out toward integrated human wholeness."[20] This is another way of saying that salvation understood in exclusively spiritual terms cannot respond to the evil of feminicide in any credible way. Arguably, salvation narrowly focused on the spiritual, at best offers a deficient understanding of salvation regardless of one's life circumstances.

If salvation is understood as the realization of wholeness and integration in the most exhaustive sense, thus on an individual and social level, then it is best understood as coming about through processes of interpretation, that is, processes of interpretation that achieve two ends. First, these processes increase the visibility of the inherent interrelatedness of all humans and all creation. Second, these processes seek out the meaning of this interrelated vision in the face of the fragmentariness and brokenness that eventually marks all life. Interpretation here is understood, above all else, as a process of integration, happening on many levels and, accordingly, not exclusively on a cognitive level. It is a process that is also affective, physical, kinesthetic, and so forth. Again, the all-encompassing integral nature of salvation is the work of the Spirit of God active in the world, animating every inclination toward human integration (personal and social) and every inclination toward recognition of the interconnectedness of all that has being.

Salvation in the shadow of feminicide must account for the extreme difference between the world as it is—one in which feminicide occurs—and the world as God desires the world to be, that is, a loving, reconciled world. Indeed, religious language about salvation must confront all that is an utter affront to what God wills for the world, in this case, the affront of feminicide. The traumatic wounds left in the wake of feminicide make the notion of a possible reconciled world seem utterly monstrous, absurd, impossible, and literally unimaginable. Here we confront the limits of human imagination. In the wake of extreme evil, how might human wholeness be advanced? Are there individuals and communities who have experienced extreme evil and yet, through their coming to terms with this experience, suggest to the rest of us a path forward, a path toward healing and integration, even more toward wholeness? Again, "It is not those innocent of evil who are fullest of the life of God, but those who in their own case have experienced the triumph over evil."[21]

The *fifth* and final guiding assertion is that salvation "in our world must address the connection between human action and the ultimate state of things, the eschaton," as Haight has argued.[22] How does human action, particularly collective human action, orient us, or not, toward the question of ultimate meaning, toward what is of ultimate value? In our time, a growing number of people have a heightened awareness of how social systems and structures privilege certain groups of individuals and marginalize other groups. Further, while evil human action has been part of the human story since the beginning of the human race, today our capacity to extend the impact of evil human action is greater than it has ever been, owing to a myriad of human scientific and technological advances. Human beings use these advances for great good and great evil.

Too often we blind ourselves to the great evil that is being done to the most vulnerable; we blind ourselves by creating a circumscribed worldview in which we distance ourselves from serious and widespread innocent suffering outside of our particular sphere.[23] Far too often, the question of meaning and value is engaged on the basis of a reduced sphere of concern and *not* on the basis of meaning and value on a global and ultimate scale. As a result, the question of *ultimate* meaning and value, because it always includes the whole interconnected world and the whole of human history, is not embraced, much less addressed. When this happens, we cling to a distorted understanding of salvation, so much so that we end up no longer talking about a Christian vision of salvation.

To be sure, salvation in the shadow of feminicide must take seriously the question of *ultimate* meaning and value. To the degree that Christians remain passive in the face of unjust social structures that make the eruption of feminicide more likely, or remain blind to what is beyond their own circumscribed world, to this degree Christians' consciousness and freedom will become attenuated and submerged. Injustices beyond their personal experiences become more of an abstraction than a reality. As a result, disciples often become less desirous of and zealous for the fullness of justice, goodness, and truth in this world and lose sight of the eschaton. Passivity or blindness to what lies beyond our particular world precipitates an obscuring of the gospel vision of the kingdom of God that Jesus Christ devoted his whole life to announcing and actualizing, a vision that provoked his crucifixion.

With these five guiding assertions to provide direction for thinking through the meaning of salvation in the shadow of feminicide, the question remains: How does Jesus mediate salvation? And how is Jesus's offer of salvation to be understood in a way that is explicit and definitive while still being "open and not exclusive"?[24]

A pneumatological Christology holds significant promise precisely because its development in Luke-Acts foregrounds God's presence in the world as constantly active, as the vivifier who gives life, as the One who ceaselessly re-creates the world, and as the One who brings "good news to the poor...release to the captives...recovery of sight to the blind...[who lets] the oppressed go free" (Luke 4:18b–19). Jesus's offer of salvation is clear, open to all, and constantly evolving as human needs for deliverance change. In the following forceful and weighty quote, Haight, with help from eminent scripture scholars, enunciates the nature and value of foregrounding a pneumatological vision of salvation and Jesus's offer of salvation as it is presented in Luke–Acts.

> The theory of salvation that is incorporated in this Spirit christology is best represented by the very term "salvation." "'Salvation' denotes the deliverance of human beings from evil, physical, moral, political, or cataclysmic. It connotes a victory, a rescue of them from a state of negation and a restoration to wholeness or integrity" [Fitzmyer]. This broad concept of salvation allows one to incorporate into it analogously the many ways in which Jesus is the agent of salvation both during his historical life and from his position as the exalted one. Jesus' offer of forgiveness of sin is salvation,

67

and Jesus' exorcism, healing, and welcoming of excluded people is salvation. In other words, Jesus' works for the integrity and humanization of people at all levels of their human existence in this world are part of God's salvation mediated by Jesus. Jesus is also savior from his position of exaltation as the one who pours out God's saving Spirit. "Indeed, Jesus' whole life is considered redemptive by Luke, for it is this agent of God who has made possible universal salvation in the community of believers through the power of the Spirit" [Richard]. Today, Jesus provides a way of pointing to the saving character of God's power of salvation present in human life and history. Salvation lies in the many effects of God's being present to human existence, and Jesus' life and resurrection reveal them [Neyrey]. Finally, the Christian life that is opened up by this christology is best characterized as discipleship. The center of attention is Jesus of Nazareth, his active life, animated by God as Spirit, directed toward the goal of the kingdom of God. This narrative christology is easily converted into the spirituality of an imitation of Christ. Discipleship engages human freedom; the kingdom of God provides a goal; the experience of grace empowers and generates courage; resurrection offers hope for the course of human existence. Finally, because this is a two-stage christology, there is a parallelism between Jesus' life and the life of other human beings, so that Jesus is imitable.[25]

This pneumatologically oriented theory of salvation is able to take seriously the challenge feminicide presents to belief in the God who saves. This theory of salvation recognizes the state of negation brought on by a serious evil such as feminicide; it foregrounds the deliverance of human beings from evil in its multiple forms; it emphasizes Jesus's role in delivering human beings from sin; it extends an offer of healing, of humanization, and of restoration of human wholeness. Moreover, it emphasizes "God's power of salvation present in human life and history."[26] All these characteristics not only locate this approach to salvation within the purview of the five guiding assertions named above, but also they pave the way for the possibility of a credible account of salvation in the shadow of feminicide.

IV

TO BELIEVE IN THE GOD WHO SAVES

"Soteriology is intrinsically narrative."[1] Simply put, human beings find themselves in some kind of negative situation or condition, they yearn for this negative situation to be transformed for the better, and at some point, they recognize their inability to secure this transformed state by means of their own efforts alone. This situation begs the question, Who or what can help humans experience the transformation they seek? Salvation's narrative structure entails the movement from the former to the latter. Above, Schillebeeckx provided clarity about the former with his phrase *negative contrast experiences*, which refers to senseless suffering brought on by injustice, suffering that is in severe conflict with a decent, humane way of experiencing the world. Negative contrast experiences seriously diminish, if not destroy, human dignity. They work against the building up of *humanum*, the dignity and flourishing of our humanness. Indeed, feminicide is an extreme example of a negative contrast experience, and it drives human beings to seek out deliverance, relief, healing, restoration, and, in time, even human flourishing.[2]

To seek a transformed existence when in the midst of the irrational, horrific evil of feminicide is to seek salvation. The narrative arc of this transformation is best understood in three moments. While Walter Brueggemann's naming of these three moments draws insightfully on the exodus event, these three moments are also present in Jesus's ministry, crucifixion-death, and resurrection.[3] The first moment is a *critique of ideology*. In Exodus, the Jews decide that they will no longer accept Pharaoh's power to enslave them. They critique their enslaved condition. In the Gospels, Jesus's ministry constantly entails an ongoing denunciation of death-dealing powers and practices, of all powers that crush life. This denunciation is always coupled with an announcement of the "already–not yet" presence of the reign of God.

The second moment is the *public processing of pain*. The Jews decide that they will no longer mourn strictly in private the pain they experience in slavery; rather, their mourning will be a public crying out against

Pharaoh, putting Pharaoh on notice that his authority is no longer legitimate. Jesus is crucified precisely because he questions the legitimacy of any dominant power—political or religious, Roman or Jewish—that rules by crushing the most vulnerable. Obviously, crying out in public carries enormous risk.

The willingness to place one's life at risk in public generates social power and, in so doing, paves the way for the third moment, namely, *the release of a new social imagination*. Along with this new imagination comes a release of energy, energy that enables the Jews to leave Pharaoh's Egypt and energy that encourages the practice of living within a transformed sense of reality. Power and energy reside in an expanded imagination that allows the human spirit to lean into freedom, to express oneself more authentically by taking on the responsibility of freedom to challenge all that attempts to crush and constrain human dignity. Following Jesus's horrific crucifixion and death, evil did not have the last word. Jesus's resurrection both reflects and encourages a new social imagination. Through Jesus's resurrection, eternity breaks into our present.

CRITIQUE OF IDEOLOGY

The prolonged, pervasive violence of feminicide takes us to a prepolitical space, meaning that the corruption and destruction of society is so pervasive that we find ourselves amid the rubble of what was once a society and in a situation in which anarchy rules and violence is the only way of addressing conflicts. Fear and terror reign. Such a space is thoroughly apocalyptic and anti-eschatological. What we find ourselves confronting is the endgame of a kyriarchal and patriarchal mindset that eventually devolves into death-dealing reign.

An awakened, critical consciousness makes possible a critique of the reigning death-dealing ideology. Ideology, as we know, is a preeminent, overarching idea accompanied by a widely held belief system that structures and guides a society, most often tacitly but always powerfully. The ideology in question is kyriarchy, which includes patriarchy but is broader in scope.[4] The presumptive world of the kyriarchal subjugation of poor brown women has sown the seeds that have led to the evil of feminicide, a social sin by every measure.

Social sin is a moral evil that is rooted in the destructive character of social beliefs, institutions, and structures with their oppressive accompanying policies and especially practices. Social sin can be particularly difficult to perceive and to dismantle. Since all beliefs, institutions, and structures are invariably the product of human freedom and since they bear a systemic, often bureaucratic character, they depend upon the choices of more than a single individual or a small group of individuals. Responsibility for social sin, while always present, is not easily deciphered. Social sin continues as the product of learned social patterns of thinking and behavior that have the effect of dehumanizing and negating human life.[5] While all societies bear some imprint of social sin, societies nonetheless vary significantly in terms of the degree to which or intensity in which social sin reigns. Feminicide is an example of the most extreme form of social sin, a social sin that has materialized within a group of people, advanced to further a social fabric of trauma and terror for the purpose of protecting the ascendency of evil and anarchy. With a state of disorder and reign of terror due to the absence or nonrecognition of authority, evil may continue unabated and unchecked. Indeed, Carlos Mendoza-Álvarez and Achille Mbembe have both urgently directed our attention to the ever-expanding reign of death-dealing power or, indeed, *necro*power. Necropower subjugates life and insists upon life lived under the constant threat of brutal violence aimed to kill.[6] Feminicide is but one example.

The social sin of feminicide makes conspicuous the urgent necessity of an insurgent theology. If Christian belief in the God who saves is to have validity and credibility in confronting feminicide, can salvation, which is the work of Jesus Christ, continue to be understood short of a thoroughgoing critique of its kyriarchal and patriarchal accretions? Indeed, the integrity of Christian soteriology weighs in the balance. A social sin, such as feminicide, requires a serious theological and ecclesial soul searching.

As a people of faith and as church, we must, in the tradition of Jesus Christ and the prophets, denounce what is dehumanizing, degrading, oppressive, negating, and destructive of human life. We must denounce what is "contrary to fellowship, justice, and liberty" because these are utterly contrary to what God wills for the human community. Gutiérrez rightly holds all would-be disciples of Jesus Christ as well as the church accountable when he issues a clarion call to the church in Latin America and, by extension, around the world:

> [The Church] must make the prophetic *denunciation* of every dehumanizing situation, which is contrary to fellowship, justice, and liberty. At the same time it must criticize every sacralization of oppressive structures to which the Church itself might have contributed. Its denunciation must be public, for its position in Latin American society is public. This denunciation may be one of the few voices— and at times the only one—which can be raised in the midst of a country submitted to repression. In this critical and creative confrontation of its faith with historical realities—a task whose roots must be in the hope in the future promised by God— the Church must go to the very causes of the situation and not be content with pointing out and attending to certain of its consequences....In Latin America this denunciation must represent a radical critique of the present order, which means that the Church must also criticize itself as an integral part of this order. This horizon will allow the Church to break out of its narrow enclosure of intraecclesial problems by placing these problems in their true

context—the total society and the broad perspective of commitment in a world of revolutionary turmoil.[7]

While Gutiérrez is speaking of the Latin American church of the late 1960s and its need to address the roots of the crushing poverty experienced by the great majority of its people, his words also ring true in the early decades of the twenty-first century with its evil scourge of feminicide. To the degree that Catholic theology fails to strip away its kyriarchal and patriarchal accretions, it offers a tacit, even if unintended, response of indifference to feminicide. Does Catholic theology have the imagination, the will, and, especially, the courage to call into question at a fundamental level the violence that destroys women's bodies, souls, and lives?

Denunciation is not complete unless and until the reality of feminicide is confronted with the *announcement* of God's overabundant love for all human beings and, in particular, for vulnerable poor brown women who have known the scourge or threat of feminicide. God's love "calls all persons in Christ and through the action of the Spirit to union among themselves and communion with [God]. To announce the Gospel is to proclaim that the love of God is present in the historical becoming of humankind."[8] Without an announcement of God's love for all human beings, the denunciation of evil rings hollow. It lacks validity. It shows up without an effective subversive vision and strategy aimed at ending evil's horrific reign. Denunciation and announcement can only ring true from within the heart of the struggle for a more just and humane world, a critique of the ideology that has led, and continues to lead, to the killing of poor brown women with impunity.

As I have argued elsewhere, everywhere feminicide has erupted, women and some men have come together to denounce this horrific evil and denounce all that lends tacit support and paves the way for the eruption of feminicide. The critique of ideology is embedded in a mire of practices of protest and resistance.[9] This is a critique of elite male power that advances the reign of death for women, a critique that demands an end to feminicide as well as to beliefs, systems, and structures that negate poor brown women's humanity and value.

Any serious critique of kyriarchy and patriarchy in soteriology must consider whether or not the salvation of women is caught in the crosshairs of the presumed significance of Jesus's maleness in most of traditional Catholic theology. As Johnson argues, much is at stake:

> Consciously or unconsciously, Jesus' maleness is lifted up and made essential for his christic function and identity, thus blocking women precisely because of their female sex from participating in the fullness of their Christian identity as images of Christ....Sexist Christology jeopardizes women's salvation, at least in theory. The Christian story

of salvation involves not only God's compassionate will to save but also the method by which this will becomes effective, namely, by God's plunging into sinful human history and transforming it from within. The early Christian axiom "What is not assumed is not redeemed, but what is assumed is saved by union with God" sums up the insight that Christ's solidarity with all of humanity is what is crucial for salvation. *"Et homo factus est,"* "and became a human being": thus does the Nicene creed confess the universal relevance of the incarnation by the use of the inclusive *homo*. But if in fact what is meant is *et vir factus est* (became a man) with stress on sexual manhood, if maleness is essential for the christic role, then women are cut out of the loop of salvation, for female sexuality is not taken on by the Word made flesh. If maleness is constitutive for the incarnation and redemption, female humanity is not assumed and therefore not saved.[10]

While Johnson did not have feminicide in mind when she wrote these words, her words nonetheless name a problem that takes on even greater theological significance when considered in the context of the reign of death that is feminicide. Moreover, the uncanny coincidence that the two countries in the world with the largest Catholic populations are also the same two countries with the highest number of feminicide victims heightens the significance of Catholic theology's response to this tragedy or the lack thereof. Without a critique of the kyriarchal and patriarchal imprint on soteriological discourse, this discourse will lack the capacity to challenge the roots of feminicide. Indeed, violence against women painfully forges a new theological space; it signals the need for a fundamentally transformed vision of salvation, a vision that locates women's bodies in the salvation imaginary. Such does not deny the maleness of the historical man Jesus, nor does it eliminate the use of male terms for God. But it does demand and privilege an expansion of the names we use to address God, and it foregrounds female terms for God. Belief in the God who saves requires a fidelity to women's bodies, a theology of habeas corpus. Indeed, we need to recognize that "salvation is finally mediated through a form of human action." As Haight justly exhorts, "Where there is no resistance to social sin, social salvation does not exist. Where there is no liberating practice in the face of social oppression, then it is nonsense to speak about salvation in this world. The language of salvation is precisely a language that appeals to freedom to make salvation happen; it is not a description of a state of affairs."[11]

Johann Baptist Metz once famously wrote,

> Looking at the situation "after Auschwitz" demands not only a painful revision of the relationship between Christians and Jews, but also a critical revision of Christian theology itself. And this is true above all for Christology, which perhaps has been the leading edge for anti-Judaism. This observation should lead us neither simply to do without Christology, nor

to a too-easy proscription of Christology. Rather, it should lead to a careful formulation of a Christology that is accountable to the situation after Auschwitz, a Christology accountable to Christians and Jews.[12]

Analogously, might Catholic theology today consider "the situation" in the midst of feminicide and seek "a careful formulation of a Christology" and soteriology that is accountable to women and the physical condition of their bodies? We have long been at the precipice of a theological inflection point. How long will it take us to recognize this? What is more, if we affirm an egalitarian anthropology but insist on an absolute and exclusive male-centric conception of Christ, then Jesus Christ does not save women. Simply put, female sexuality is not assumed in the incarnation. And we are left with a deep fissure in our theological thinking. But if female sexuality is assumed in the incarnation, then our conception of Christ is necessarily more expansive. Such a more expansive conception of Christ might very well point us toward a pneumatological Christology.

PUBLIC PROCESSING OF PAIN

Surviving family members and friends know the extreme and manifold pain caused by feminicide and know the overwhelming experience of this pain—so much so that the temptation may be to withdraw to a solitary place to wail and grieve with only the closest

81

of family members. To take on more may be unimaginable, if not impossible.

Yet, to express this pain in public (such as with protests, marches, memorial installations, and actions calling out public officials) with the intent of drawing attention to feminicide's horrific destruction of humanity and to the corrupt, dominant civil authority that turns a blind eye to feminicide, this public act serves to delegitimize dominant power, and, as such, is a subversive act. This public act carries enormous risk precisely due to its subversive intent. It is an act that resists feminicide and demands its immediate cessation and justice for its victims.[13] When pain is experienced privately and each sufferer experiences their pain in isolation, then no social power can be generated. To cry out in public not only generates social power—it likewise is an insurgent act; it is a challenge to the reigning authority; it is the first step in forging a countercommunity, one that dismantles the old way of doing things, one that creates a new way of perceiving reality, a transformed sense of reality.

Feminicide, at once a pervasive evil and a social sin, calls into question the adequacy of understandings of salvation that are exclusively or even primarily individualistic. To ask what it means to believe in the God who saves when we find ourselves confronted with the eruption and escalation of feminicide is even more ominous, because this evil is most pervasive in countries with the greatest number of Catholic faithful.

This line of thought necessarily situates this study of salvation in the realm of political theology.

> Political theology...interprets God and God's salvation in its relevance to human beings in society and their exercise of political responsibility. On the one hand, political theology reacts against an individualistic existential interpretation of human existence and the salvation offered it. On the other hand, it proposes a social, historical anthropology as a lever for lifting up the meaning of Christian salvation in its bearing on the whole Christian community and society generally, but with special attention to the victims of society who suffer and are marginalized. Political theology brings together hermeneutical theory and critical social theory into a creative reinterpretation of the latent emancipatory themes of Christian tradition.[14]

The public processing of pain is an exercise of political responsibility. Would-be disciples of Jesus Christ must be about just this kind of work. In Copeland's words, "To follow the tears of a crucified world, the tears and weeping of a crucified people, is to arrive at the foot of the cross—the place where a disciple must stand, must take a stand rooted in knowing and loving Christ crucified."[15]

Moreover, the public processing of pain serves the purpose of recovering public space. For even the dead themselves have a right to speak and to be heard.

Our religious rituals teach us as much and so do the communities of survivors when they keep alive the memories of their loved ones unjustly and brutally murdered. When the communities of survivors keep alive the dangerous memories of innocent victims, these memories unsettle and disturb us through their capacity to provoke critical questions about the present. Such critical questions interrogate any temptation to a narrow focus on reason alone and thus to any inclination to circumscribe hope. Societal forces, and often our faith, endeavor to suppress dangerous memories so that the political, social, and even ecclesial status quo is not in any way threatened or called into question.[16] Yet, in our time, presses Althaus-Reid, "the bodies of women, and specifically of marginalized women in church and society, have reappeared in theological discourse to produce a crisis, a crisis in the sense of God's judgment upon the patriarchal ideologies, which have sadly pervaded Christian theology, a theology that silenced the multitudes."[17]

Dangerous memories when brought forward in public rites and symbols have a great regenerative power, power unleashed to re-create the world anew.

The rites and religious symbols in memory of the disappeared or of people killed by the necropower make visible in a collective way—recovering public space, often kidnapped by criminal mafias of all kinds—the will to life of...communities of survivors....In short, the celebration of Life is the spiritual dimension of epistemological and active practices of resistance that refuse to accept death as the last word on people who are excluded, discriminated against, disappeared or killed. Therefore, there is nothing more political—in the most radical and anarchic sense of the term—than a celebration of the dead as living, located in the remembrance of the community of survivors. And, thus, "hope against all hope" makes its way...(Rom 4:18).[18]

Mendoza-Álvarez knows firsthand that a "celebration of the dead as living" is all the more potent in communities decimated by the ongoing killing of the innocent and the young. Grieving communities have much to teach about what being alive means.

The eruptions of feminicide around the globe and particularly in Latin America have unleashed numerous public protests and public demands that these killings cease immediately and that the perpetrators be brought to justice for their heinous acts. In the mid-1990s, upon detecting a pattern in the assassinations of increasing numbers of women in Ciudad Juárez, mothers, activists, and other protesters there began calling the world's attention to this horrific form of evil. These leaders raised the world's consciousness of the phenomenon of feminicide, which in turn helped others to identity feminicide when it erupted in their regions of the world. In Ciudad Juárez, protesters used the symbol of the cross, painted pink, in their public protests, marches, and memorials. Among Christian faithful, the cross is typically painted in a neutral color (brown, black, gray, silver, or gold), making it jarring to see the cross painted pink.

Regular public protests have been and are a widespread practice that makes use of religious symbols to claim public space, and to claim public time in imaginative ways. Over the years, pink crosses have become so widely used that they have become an iconic symbol of resistance to feminicide not only in Ciudad Juárez, but also in Guatemala City; in Buenos Aires, Argentina; in San Pedro Sula, Honduras; in Santiago, Chile, among many other locales. For example, as a way to claim public space, in the late 1990s in Ciudad Juárez, the activist group Voces sin Eco started painting crosses on electric poles and telephone poles throughout the city. One pole was painted for every woman or girl assassinated, to both keep her *presente*, visible in public, and to protest this tragic social evil. As the tragedy of feminicide grew, protestors painted more and more poles with crosses. Also, in Ciudad Juárez a large installation of a pink cross has been erected at one of the international bridges that typically sees tens of thousands of people regularly crossing back and forth between the United States and Mexico. Officials have taken it down from time to time, not wanting the installation to discourage tourism and commerce. Protestors re-erect it each time, thereby laying claim to a public space. "In countries like Guatemala, Brazil and Mexico, an initiative has taken place to create special public transportation for women only, where they are free from threats and sexual harassment. This is especially effective against organized crime related femicide, because this usually takes place in public places or at least outside the home."[19]

Protestors have laid claim to time and space in public. For example, in Santiago and in Buenos Aires, activists there have organized large groups of women and girls to occupy a large sector of the central city plaza and demonstrate by engaging in synchronized movement done in unison with an extended chant of protest against feminicide.[20] Protestors have also laid claim to time publicly when they organize protest marches on days that recognize female humanity (e.g., March 8, International Women's Day; November 25, International Day for the Elimination of Violence against Women; and Mother's Day), and these protest marches use a religious symbol such as the cross painted pink to protest feminicide. Moreover, the murdered women's or girls' names are frequently painted on the crosses' crossbars, recognizing each individual human person murdered. In using a symbol like the cross, there is an extended temporal connection being made between the assassinations of women today (feminicide) and the assassination of Jesus Christ almost two thousand years ago.[21] These public practices of resistance or protest recognize the personal and social trauma that continues to grip communities in so many countries, and they serve as a social outcry aimed not only at civil authorities but also at God.

These protests became, and continue to be, a political and theological interruption.

The public processing of pain always involves significant risk precisely because it is public. To protest against and therefore subvert the evil of feminicide, refusing to allow this evil to have the last word, such action affirms that there is a limit to evil. This is dangerous work, and it has cost activists, protestors, investigators, and journalists their lives. Norma Andrade is a bereaved mother who decided to speak out publicly against feminicide. She lost her seventeen-year-old daughter, Lilia Alejandra García Andrade, to feminicide in 2001 in Ciudad Juárez. As a vehicle to protest these killings, to demand that they end, and to seek justice for their daughters, Norma Andrade founded a group, Nuestras Hijas de Regreso a Casa.[22] In 2011, she was shot five times and miraculously survived. She then moved to Mexico City where she was again attacked, this time by a man who slashed her face. Activists believe she was targeted for her work of documenting the hundreds of unsolved murders of women in Ciudad Juárez, including that of her daughter. No doubt, those who have protested this horror have placed their own lives at risk. Andrade's work, along with that of many others, is "a course of action at the service of the resurrection of the dead."[23] Andrade's work is so that others might live. Her own excruciating suffering resulting from the brutal assassination of her daughter and from her own injuries has compelled her to see that there are still other daughters and families at risk. Through her courageous leadership, these others, almost all of whom she will never know personally, are less likely to suffer as she has suffered. Through her courageous work, Andrade exemplifies that it "is not those innocent of evil who are fullest of the life of God, but those who in their own case have experienced the triumph over evil"[24]—and done so at great personal cost. While we can never fully rid the world of evil, we can subordinate it.

Persons like Andrade, whether they realize it or not, are prophets who pave the way for the rest of us to catch a glimpse of the eschatological in the midst of overwhelming evil that denies the very possibility of God's future. The glimpse of the eschatological emerges because persons like Andrade willingly risk their own lives on behalf of life by fighting against feminicide and thereby creating conditions such that God's presence in history becomes more transparently visible, and such that the graced nature of female humanity becomes more wholly honored. Copeland must have had people like Andrade in mind when she preached,

> Certainly, in Latin America and in Africa—and in so many parts of our crucified world—the political, economic, and technological conditions of ordinary people represent grievous sin and evil. We have crucified these poor, excluded, and despised children, women, and men through corrupt consciences and crooked systems. Yet, these crucified

people are the only sure sign of God's presence in our world. For these children, women, and men offer us a graced and saving encounter with God's mercy, compassion, and love. These are our brothers and sisters, members of Jesus's own family. They are our partners and companions in the work of justice; together, side by side, we struggle to find out what it means to live "the way" of Jesus. Only together, side by side, we glimpse the promised parousia.[25]

What we learn here is that a glimpse of the eschatological requires an expansion of our imagination in directions uncomfortable, that is, alongside those we have crucified, recognizing that these crucified persons have much to teach us about God's mercy and salvation.

However, the public processing of pain must involve further steps that carry their own risks. How might we, the disciples of Christ, name this tragedy so that we situate ourselves within its purview? So that it impacts our way of talking about God? In our own time, amid its many challenges, might the increasing number of feminicide victims who have been stripped of their humanity and their lives, might these tortured and murdered human beings be the crucified people of our time? The theological plight of the feminicide victims is as a crucified people. "This crucified people represents the historical continuation of the servant of Yahweh, who is forever being stripped of his human features by the sin of the world, who is forever being despoiled of everything by the powerful of this world, who is forever being robbed of life, especially of life."[26] It is risky to expand our understanding of the crucifixion of Jesus Christ so that it includes murdered, poor brown women and girls. Indeed, feminicide victims and survivors ask of us not only to look carefully and closely at the relationship between women and men, between brown and white, between the poor and the wealthy, but to consider a revision of how we talk about God. What does it mean to speak of "a crucified people" when the crucifixion is an act of feminicide?

In addition to the public practices named in the preceding paragraphs, theological discourse can further mediate the public processing of pain. What follows in the remainder of this section is an attempt at this kind of mediation. If the victims of feminicide are identified as a crucified people, what might this mean? How might this be theologically significant? What does such an identification challenge? What is the risk? To what degree does such an identification expand our theological imaginations toward the good? And to what degree does this encourage the in-breaking of God's future into our present?

Two questions launch this mediation. What does the phrase *a crucified people* signify? And what does it mean to identify the victims of feminicide as a crucified people? A great portion of humanity knows crucifixion as their historical reality. The historical reality of ongoing crucifixions is the direct result of human decisions and structures.

As Ignacio Ellacuría explains,

[A] "crucified people"...is a...collective body...[that] owes its situation of crucifixion to the way society is organized and maintained by a minority....[This minority] exercises its dominion through a series of factors, which taken together and given their concrete impact within history, must be regarded as sin.[27]

Thus, a crucified people is not simply people who know suffering but a particular group who suffer because of their *shared historical reality*, their collective vulnerability. The victims exemplify a group "from whom the sin of the world continues to take away all human form, and whom the powers of this world dispossess of everything, seizing even their lives, above all their lives."[28]

To identify the feminicide victims as a crucified people carries several meanings, each signifying the theological gravity of these assassinations. *First,* such identification affirms that we, the followers of Jesus, must not view Jesus's crucifixion in isolation from the assassinations of innocent victims throughout history. If we do not make this connection, then the suffering of the innocent is, without a doubt, trivialized, if not completely ignored. Ivone Gebara has argued as much:

Indeed, Jesus of Nazareth, proclaimed the Christ by the community of believers, keeps his cross as a distinctive and unique sign. We are not denying this personal and historic aspect. But...this cross is not greater or lesser than others, even though it is a cross of an innocent man. It surely represents a reference to a community of faith, but it must be set in dialogue with others if it is to avoid manipulation.[29]

When we link the particularity of Jesus's crucifixion to that of today's victims of feminicide, we hold ourselves accountable for the abuse of power in our time. We step closer to confronting our blindness, the ways in which our own group interests function to limit our intelligence and circumscribe the range of our insight.[30] My point is that the meaning of "a crucified people" cannot be engaged exclusively, or even primarily, at a symbolic, figurative, or metaphorical level but must be acutely focused on the material level, in this case on the bodies of women being crucified today. Short of this, we participate in the abuse of power that leads to such evil.

Second, to refer to those victimized by feminicide as a crucified people is to shine a spotlight on the much greater vulnerability of women at high risk for the violence of feminicide, among other forms of violence women suffer. By their identity markers as women, as brown, and as poor, those victimized by feminicide form a collective body who are vulnerable to the whims of dominant society acting in its own self-interests, for economic, political, social, or even simply capricious reasons. A small sector of society— those in positions of power and dominance—operate as a force to bend history in their own direction. This is sin. Frequently, the vulnerability of women is exacerbated and institutionalized through the perverted but prevalent interpretation of religious symbols that tacitly provide justification for the enduring subordination of women. In describing a common understanding of the cross among poor women in Latin America, Gebara protests:

> The cross is identified with their suffering and a kind of curse—being born female. This idea is deeply rooted in the popular culture of Latin America. The fate of being female is often considered a misfortune....[For a group of] women from poor neighborhoods in Recife...the cross was not just the suffering of their daily lives in poverty but also their condition as women. Christianity taught them to bear and even welcome their cross rather than to look for ways to be rid of it.[31]

This sinful legacy has lent support for the assassinations of women. However, to place feminicide victims at the center of our soteriological vision transforms and expands our understanding of the cross and crucifixion. We are thus encouraged to ask not only *who* is crucifying these women but also *what* is crucifying them. To what degree do commonplace understandings of the cross encourage us to turn a blind eye to this tragedy? And, conversely, what kind of understandings of the cross and crucifixion encourage us, the disciples of Christ, to work so that feminicide is no more?

Third, when we consider those victimized by feminicide as a crucified people, we recognize that the tragedy of this crucifixion is brought about by social, structural sin. Fundamentally, hegemonic, economic, sociopolitical power—forged by neoliberal capitalism, patriarchy, kyriarchy, colonialism, and religious views that uncritically idealize suffering—has led to large numbers of people living in extreme poverty and desperation, a context ripe for the eruption of feminicide. The crucifixion that is feminicide interrogates any acquiescence we who are disciples of Jesus might feel toward a so-called benevolent patriarchy. A "benevolent" patriarchy coupled with economic desperation far too easily slips toward what eventually becomes an evil like feminicide. However, when we hold our thinking about God accountable to the gospel message of liberation for the downtrodden, the captive, the oppressed, and the forgotten (Luke 4:18), we walk down the path of bringing the crucified victims of feminicide down from the cross. Identifying feminicide victims as a crucified people nudges us one step further along the path of justice.

While feminicide is, without a doubt, an example of social, structural sin, acknowledging as much always presents a significant challenge. If sin as well as salvation are considered exclusively as privatized and individual concerns, then it is much more straightforward to note a moral failing or sin and to clarify who is responsible for their action or inaction. Of course, social sin and structural evil have actors, but it is far more difficult to clarify all the parties responsible, their roles in the action or inaction, and to parse out the fault or failing. Social sin and structural evil have a bureaucratic character. It can be multigenerational. It can be strongly advanced through conventional and reigning ways of thinking in which many of the actors are, to varying degrees, blind to the sinful impact of their actions or inactions. Social sin and structural evil are often part of the air we breathe, which is indeed the case when we consider racism, colonialism, sexism, classism, homophobia, and so forth. Sinful ways of thinking become so normalized that they easily slip by unnoticed unless, of course, you are a person who is directly harmed by these ways of thinking. And even then, there are large portions of oppressed populations who have so internalized racist and sexist ways of thinking that they themselves live life in a state of intrapersonal existential alienation, cut off from their authentic selves.

Fourth, and finally, this identification urges a critique of the presumption that maleness is more essential to divinity than femaleness. Far too often Jesus, the cross, and crucifixion have been grossly distorted with interpretations that serve to legitimate male dominance in the human community. Implicit in this kind of interpretation is the idea that the maleness of Jesus is integral and essential to "his christic function and identity."[32] Accordingly, this means that women by virtue of their femaleness cannot participate in the "fullness of their Christian identity as images of Christ."[33] This flawed theological interpretation provides an ultimate justification for gendered gradations in humanity with disastrous consequences.

Far too often, Christians have wrongly argued that because Jesus was a man, maleness and divinity are ontologically interrelated in a manner that cannot exist between femaleness and divinity. Since Jesus was a man, and God chose to be incarnated in a man, then men have a divinely ordained superiority over women. This line of thinking forecloses preemptively the possibility that God could have become incarnate in a female human being. What is at issue here is whether we believe that Christ became a human being (as is stated in the Nicene Creed) or that Christ became a man. The protests against feminicide confront and explode this kind of ontological approach to the relationship between maleness and divinity and point us toward a very different interpretation.

The tradition of Catholic social teaching, with its consistent affirmation of the dignity of all human persons, would have us ask, What understandings of the cross and crucifixion support misogyny? What understandings of the cross and crucifixion dismantle misogyny? Nothing is more urgent for Christian believers than to develop answers to these questions. We need to know not only *who* is killing the women, but also *what* is killing them. By this I refer to the distorted "theological" thinking that undermines the full dignity of female humanity.

When confronted with feminicide we, Jesus's followers, must ask ourselves whether we believe that another world is possible. If so, what are we willing to risk to bring about another world? The public processing of pain always requires great risk. Through our embracing of the risk, we generate social power and energy. This social power and energy make possible the release of a new social imagination, thus leading to the re-creation of the world. Further, this energy funds the social practice of living within a transformed sense of reality.

The next and final moment evolves from the first two. While the three moments represent the narrative character of salvation, they do not evolve in a strictly linear or sequential manner. The in-breaking of salvation in human history is more of an art than a science, more messy than neat and tidy.

RELEASE OF A NEW SOCIAL IMAGINATION

Everything we create is created twice: first, mentally in our imagination, and second, materially. No less than Albert Einstein once preached, "I am enough of an artist to draw freely upon my imagination.

Imagination is more important than knowledge. For knowledge is limited, whereas imagination encircles the world."[34]

Our capacity to re-create the world in a way that reaches toward Jesus's vision of the reign of God deepens and expands when we flex the power of our imaginations. Living as if another world is possible, what Roberto Goizueta once called life in the subjunctive, is what Jesus's disciples are called to cultivate, nurture, and make real in history.[35] Always, there will be attempts by established power and authority to "privatize and reduce" the new emerging social imagination, to crush the new transformed sense of reality. The endeavor to re-create the world by influencing the contours of social, public space by holding sway in the arena of public authority, these efforts to nudge our common social life in the direction of greater justice is inevitably fraught with high tension and amplified conflict.

Yet always there is great power in the vision of a transformed sense of reality. The poor, the downtrodden, the oppressed, and the family survivors of feminicide, these persons often have an uncanny sense of the power in the vision of transformed reality. The Holy Spirit unceasingly speaks through the prophetic voices of these marginalized peoples. For the disciples of Jesus who are listening, these prophetic voices offer inspiration to re-create the world, to recognize salvation breaking into the present, and to affirm the credibility of resurrection hope.

Through their own public acts of resistance, the family survivors of feminicide are living into a transformed sense of reality, that is, a sense of reality that intensifies the visibility of God's presence in history. These survivors are much like the bent-over woman of Luke's Gospel who has been told to stand upright (Luke 13:10–17); they, too, are hearing the call to stand upright. Or like the Syrophoenician woman of Matthew's Gospel who invites Jesus to imagine for himself a more inclusive understanding of his mission (Matt 15:21–28), the survivors, too, are calling all disciples of Jesus to imagine for themselves a more commanding appreciation of the value of female human persons. These biblical passages signal an eschatological provisionality; they call our attention to God's future breaking into human history, into our present. What matters above all else is God's promised future. Nowhere is this more evident than in the biblical passages that call our attention to the empty tomb.

The "empty tomb" tradition of the Gospels, especially that of Matthew (28:1–10) and Mark (15:47—16:11), offers us an account of Jesus's whereabouts that requires more than a confession of faith in Jesus's resurrection. This tradition requires a response of action. By way of contrast, the "appearance" tradition in the Gospels evokes a response of a confession of faith but not necessarily a response of action. Elisabeth Schüssler Fiorenza urges us to consider that "the proclamation of the empty tomb locates the Resurrected One on earth, in Galilee. Resurrection means that Jesus, the

Living One, goes ahead of us."[36] Matthew and Mark both underscore the import of Jesus being here in our midst, here on earth, but ahead of us. While both Luke and John have an account of the empty tomb, they have Jesus ascending to heaven and not on the open road. Matthew's account, in particular, connects "the visionary experience of the Resurrected One with the 'open space' of the empty tomb and the 'open road' pointing ahead to Galilee. It also entrusts the resurrection proclamation to the witness of women. It insists on the bodily materiality of resurrection and the vindication of unjust suffering and death with the assertion that the tomb is 'empty.'"[37]

This empty tomb tradition creates a liminal space that encourages recognition of the experience of survivors of feminicide. These family survivors find themselves living in a liminal space between despair and hope, in a space of overwrought rage or exhausted numbness at the injustice of misogynistic evil. The space of the empty tomb is pregnant with ambiguity, which affords it the capaciousness to hold the breadth and depth of the horror of feminicide. Indeed, as Schüssler Fiorenza continues, "The texts of the empty tomb tradition take suffering and death seriously but do not see them as having the 'last word' or a religious-theological value in themselves. Since G*d was absent in the execution of the Just One, the women's presence under the cross is a witness to this absence. The tomb is the brutal final reality that eclipses G*d and vitiates all possibilities for the future. But the 'tomb

101

is empty!'"[38] The empty tomb means that Jesus, who was crucified, is now living, opening up a new path for us. God did not permit the horrific assassination of the innocent Jesus to have the last word; in Jesus's resurrection, we find a limit to evil. If we believe that Jesus is the Living One who goes ahead of us, then, might those victimized by feminicide, those murdered and their surviving family members, also have hope in a future vindication, in a "resurrection reality"?

Such hope, born of a new social imagination, further introduces and requires *a much-expanded vision of reality*, one that appreciates that the significance of our lives obviously includes, but extends well beyond, our lifetimes. This expanded vision deepens the transformed sense of reality mentioned above. With this expanded vision, the significance of our lives extends into the distant *past* to include Jesus's life story as our own story, with all his joys and sorrows. And, the significance of our lives extends into the distant hoped-for *future* of the Parousia, Jesus's second coming, which we anticipate as our very own future. Thus, we live in the present always mindful of this distant past and future. An expanded vision of reality must likewise have been what the first disciples came to appreciate over the course of their lives:

Before their Easter experience, as far as the disciples were concerned, Jesus remained dead. What they had hoped for, whatever their confused religious expectations might have been, seemed to be shattered by the sudden and sheerly definitive power of death. The Easter experience reverses this despair and fills an empty void....In terms of salvation, the resurrection of Jesus opens up a new dimension of reality for these disciples. The future now becomes a real dimension of being for the person who transcends living "only in order to die." One can imagine in the disciples a passage from religious or cosmic despair to a fundamental conviction characterized by hope.[39]

This expanded vision of reality connects the ways we each live our life in the here and now to the ultimate meaning and value that God intends, the eschaton. The larger significance of our lives becomes provisionally realized in the *present*, an expression of realized eschatology.

This much-expanded vision of reality is visible in the prophetic actions of women like Andrade. Even though nothing she could do would bring her daughter back to her as she had known her before and nothing could erase her memory of her daughter's utterly brutal assassination, still Andrade worked to subvert the evil of feminicide at great risk to herself as a life work on behalf of other families she did not know personally, and on behalf of the ascendency of the good in this world. She recognized that her life has a much larger significance than what she will know in her lifetime. Andrade is not alone. There are many women and some men who have lost their daughters and engaged in work similar to Andrade's. This life work exemplifies living as if another world is possible and affirms in the strongest possible way that another world is not only possible but is breaking into our present.

The resurrection reality mentioned here is born of a sober hope and not optimism. Without a doubt, the powers of the world will find this different vision of reality threatening. Change is unwanted by those who control the levers of the economy, society, and the political sphere. Neoliberal capitalism, patriarchy, colonialism, and religious ideas that uncritically valorize suffering—all of these overarching systems and beliefs come together and coalesce to normalize the world as it is even with its reign of death, and, by extension, the beneficiaries of this reign of death endlessly seek to reduce and privatize any upstart new social imagination. Invariably conflicts sharpen and even become lethal around which persons and what overarching systems and beliefs will exercise a controlling and normalizing function in the public space. The attempts on Andrade's life clearly demonstrate as much. Jesus's own life, as presented in the Gospel of Luke, also illustrates this persistent conflict:

"And all spoke highly of him and were amazed at the gracious words that came from his mouth" (4:22). But when Jesus recalls incidents associated with the prophets Elijah and Elisha, in which God's visitation was extended to Gentiles outside the boundaries of Israel, the tide quickly turns. The crowd tries to drive him out of town, leading him to "the brow of the hill" (4:29)—a hill that becomes symbolic of the hill of Calvary. There will be no favoritism in the mission of Jesus. One of the reasons that Jesus will not be accepted in his native country is that the Spirit will impel him to extend his mission beyond his own people.[40]

Might this same Spirit be impelling us, his followers, to extend his mission beyond the limits of overarching systems and beliefs that fail to recognize women, especially poor women of color, as human beings and, for many, Jesus Christ's disciples in the fullest sense?

Feminicide poses a particularly acute challenge to Christian conceptions of salvation. Will these conceptions of salvation evolve both to affirm the singular role of Jesus as mediator of salvation and, at the same time, to dismantle any and all kyriarchal, patriarchal accretions and distortions so commonplace in Christian conceptions of salvation? Jesus's ministry continuously affirmed that the reign of God has been, and can be, partially realized in specific communities in concrete historical situations. Indeed, Jesus spent his life in service of an ever-greater realization of the reign of God in a specific historical situation. What endures in every historical situation is the struggle to realize the reign of God over and against the reign of death in its multitudinous expressions. The success of this struggle is always a matter of degree, a struggle ultimately waged on the stage of God's eschatological horizon. Today feminicide places women and Catholic theology at the center of this struggle. What does it mean to believe in the God who saves?

NOTES

INTRODUCTION

1. I am grateful to the following individuals for their advice and support as I wrote this book: Nancy de Flon; Arlene Montevecchio; Francine Cardman; Larry Gordon; John Markey, Rosemary Carbine, Rafael Luevano; and Mary Lowe. I am grateful to Megan Heeder for her work as my research assistant.

2. Alan Greig, "Doing Gender Differently: Transforming Masculinity," United Nations Development Program (UNDP), posted April 16, 2021, https://www.undp.org/blogs/doing-gender-differently-transforming-masculinity.

3. For an insightful discussion of this challenge, see Robert J. Daly, "Images of God and the Imitation of God: Problems with Atonement," *Theological Studies* 68 (2007): 36–51.

4. "UN Expert Calls for Urgent Action to End 'Pandemic of Femicide and Violence against Women,'" United Nations News Global Perspective Human Stories, November 23, 2020, https://news.un.org/en/story/2020/11/1078362; "Understanding and Addressing Violence against Women: Femicide," World Health Organization (WHO), 2012, http://apps.who.int/iris/bitstream/handle/10665/77421/WHO_RHR_12.38

_eng.pdf;jsessionid=B7D7D23413A7474740C494747C686B59
?sequence=1.

5. With very rare exceptions, women are not killing women because they are women. And with rare exceptions, women are not killing men simply because they are men.

6. See Nancy Pineda-Madrid, *Suffering and Salvation in Ciudad Juárez* (Minneapolis: Fortress Press, 2011), 11–12, 26–27. Note that in this short book, you will see primarily *feminicide* and occasionally *femicide*. Both refer to the killing of women because they are women. *Feminicide* refers to assassinations in very large numbers, while *femicide* can mean the assassination of only one woman or girl. Scholars are not of one mind regarding which term to use. Some scholars do use *femicide* and mean more than one assassination. In this book, I have chosen to favor *feminicide* and only use *femicide* when that is the word used in a given quote.

I. GIVING RISE TO THE QUESTION OF SALVATION

1. *Negative contrast experience* is a term coined by Edward Schillebeeckx and, according to Kathleen McManus, it "refers to those experiences of injustice, oppression, and suffering that give rise to protest and the ethical imperative toward active transformation." See Kathleen McManus, "Suffering in the Theology of Edward Schillebeeckx," *Theological Studies* 60 (1999): 477.

2. Roger Haight, *Jesus Symbol of God* (Maryknoll, NY: Orbis, 1999), 355.

3. Paul Tillich, *Systematic Theology*, vol. 1 (Chicago: University of Chicago Press, 1951), 81–82, 165–66, 190–210.

4. Josiah Royce, *The Sources of Religious Insight* (New York: Charles Scribner's Sons, 1912), 262, 49, 259.

5. Richard Bernstein, *Radical Evil: A Philosophical Investigation* (Malden, MA: Blackwell Publishers, 2002), 228.

6. Claudio Marcelo Viale, "Royce and Bernstein on Evil," *Contemporary Pragmatism* 10, no. 1 (June 2013): 82.

7. Hannah Arendt, *The Jew as Pariah: Jewish Identity and Politics in the Modern Age* (New York: Grove Press, 1978), 251.

8. Charles Taylor, *Modern Social Imaginaries* (Durham, NC: Duke University Press, 2004), 23.

9. Emilie Townes, *Womanist Ethics and the Cultural Production of Evil* (New York: Palgrave Macmillan, 2006).

10. As quoted in Frank M. Oppenheim, *Royce's Mature Ethics* (Notre Dame, IN: University of Notre Dame Press, 1993), 42.

11. Royce, *Sources of Religious Insight*, 12.

12. Royce, *Sources of Religious Insight*, 17, 38, 171, 174, 259.

13. Royce, *Sources of Religious Insight*, 53, 33.

14. Haight, *Jesus Symbol of God*, 354.

15. Haight, *Jesus Symbol of God*, 355. See also 214–15, 336, 339.

16. Haight, *Jesus Symbol of God*, 339.

II. VIOLENCE AGAINST
WOMEN AS WOMEN

1. "The VPA Approach," World Health Organization (WHO) Violence Prevention Alliance, accessed December 13, 2021, https://www.who.int/groups/violence-prevention-alliance/approach.

2. John D. Carlson, "Religion and Violence: Coming to Terms with Terms," in *The Blackwell Companion to Religion*

and Violence, ed. Andrew R. Murphy (Malden, MA: Blackwell Publishing, 2011), 15–17.

3. "Crimes Against Humanity," United Nations Office on Genocide Prevention and the Responsibility to Protect, accessed July 15, 2020, https://www.un.org/en/genocideprevention/crimes-against-humanity.shtml.

4. Pascha Bueno-Hansen, "Feminicidio: Making the Most of an 'Empowered Term,'" in *Terrorizing Women: Feminicide in the Américas*, ed. Rosa-Linda Fregoso and Cynthia Bejarano (Durham, NC: Duke University Press, 2010), 290–311; Jorge Alonso, "Marcela Lagarde: A Feminist Battles Feminicide," *Envio—Información sobre Nicaragua y Centroamérica*, no. 286 (May 2005), https://www.envio.org.ni/articulo/2934; still other scholars use the term *femicide*. See, e.g., Diana E. H. Russell, "The Origin and the Importance of the Term Femicide," December 2011, accessed July 15, 2020, https://www.dianarussell.com/origin_of_femicide.html. *Femicide* is synonymous with homicide except that it refers to the killing of women exclusively. Like a homicide, it can be used to refer to one murder.

5. Bueno-Hansen, "Feminicidio," 293.

6. In the late 1980s, feminist theologians Mary Daly and Jane Caputi used the term *gynocide* to identify the crime of killing women because they are women. They defined *gynocide* as "the fundamental intent of global patriarchy: planned, institutionalized spiritual and bodily destruction of women; the use of deliberate systematic measures (such as killing, bodily or mental injury, unlivable conditions, prevention of births), which are calculated to bring about the destruction of women as a political and cultural force, the eradication of Female/Bio-logical religion and language, and ultimately the extermination of the Race of Women

and all Elemental being; the master model of genocide; paradigm for the systematic destruction of any racial, political, or cultural group." See Mary Daly and Jane Caputi, *Websters' First New Intergalactic Wickedary of the English Language* (Boston: Beacon Press, 1987), 77.

7. Nancy Pineda-Madrid, *Suffering and Salvation in Ciudad Juárez* (Minneapolis: Fortress Press, 2011), 19–68.

8. Susan Brooks Thistlethwaite, *Women's Bodies as Battlefield: Christian Theology and the Global War on Women* (New York: Palgrave Macmillan, 2015), 3.

9. See, e.g., Suzannah Lipscomb, "A Very Brief History of Witches," *History Extra*, accessed July 15, 2020, https://www.historyextra.com/period/history-witches-facts-burned-hanged/.

10. Many theologians today are examining trauma and theology. See, e.g., Shelly Rambo, *Spirit and Trauma: A Theology of Remaining* (Louisville, KY: Westminster John Knox, 2010); Annie Selak, "Toward an Ecclesial Vision in the Shadow of Wounds" (PhD diss., Boston College, 2020); Karen O'Donnell and Katie Cross, eds., *Feminist Trauma Theologies: Body, Scripture & Church in Critical Perspective* (London: SCM Press, 2020).

11. "Femicide: A Global Problem," *Small Arms Survey Research Notes* 14 (February 2012), https://smallarmssurvey.org/resource/femicide-global-problem-research-note-14.

12. "Femicide and International Women's Rights: An Epidemic of Violence in Latin America," *The Global Americans Report*, 2020, https://theglobalamericans.org/reports/femicide-international-womens-rights/.

13. "Feminicidio," Observatorio de Igualdad de Género de América Latina y el Caribe, Naciones Unidas—Comisión

Económica para América Latina y el Caribe (CEPAL), https://oig.cepal.org/es/indicadores/feminicidio.

14. Michelle Bachelet, "Opening Message," in *Femicide: A Global Issue That Demands Action*, ed. Claire Laurent, Michael Platzer, and Maria Idomir (Academic Council on the United Nations System [ACUNS] Vienna Liaison Office, 2013), 6, http://www.genevadeclaration.org/fileadmin/docs/Co-publications/Femicide_A%20Gobal%20Issue%20that%20demands%20Action.pdf.

15. Jon Sobrino, "Spirituality and the Following of Jesus," in *Mysterium Liberationis: Fundamental Concepts of Liberation Theology*, ed. Ignacio Ellacuría and Jon Sobrino (Maryknoll, NY: Orbis Books, 1993), 681.

16. Sobrino, "Spirituality and the Following of Jesus," 681.

17. A number of theologians make this same point. See, e.g., Ivone Gebara, *Out of the Depths: Women's Experience of Evil and Salvation* (Minneapolis: Fortress Press, 2002); Marcella María Althaus-Reid, "¿Bién Sonados? The Future of Mystical Connections in Liberation Theology," *Political Theology* 3 (2000): 44–63; Virginia Raquel Azcuy, "Una Expresión de un Signo de Estos Tiempos: Mapas de Teología Feminista Cristiana," in *Teología Feminista a Tres Voces*, ed. V. R. Azcuy, N. E. Bedford, and M. L. García Bachmann (Santiago de Chile: Ediciones Universidad Alberto Hurtado, 2016); María Pilar Aquino, *Our Cry for Life: Feminist Theology from Latin America* (Maryknoll, NY: Orbis Books, 1993); María Pilar Aquino and M. J. Rosado-Nunes, eds., *Feminist Intercultural Theology: Latina Explorations for a Just World* (Maryknoll, NY: Orbis Books, 2007).

18. Anastasia Moloney, "Colombia Confronts Femicide, the 'Most Extreme Form of Violence against Women,'"

Reuters, August 19, 2015, https://www.reuters.com/article/
us-colombia-women-murder/colombia-confronts-femicide
-the-most-extreme-form-of-violence-against-women
-idUSKCN0QP0CM20150820.

19. Marcela Lagarde y De Los Rios, "Preface: Feminist
Keys for Understanding Feminicide; Theoretical, Political,
and Legal Construction," in *Terrorizing Women: Feminicide in
the Americas*, ed. Rosa-Linda Fregoso and Cynthia Bejarano
(Durham, NC: Duke University Press, 2010): xi–xxv. Also, see
explanation in intro., n. 6 above.

20. My 2011 book is the first theology book to address
the evil tragedy of feminicide as it erupted in Ciudad Juárez.
Prior to my work, there were several social science books
addressing feminicide that I cite extensively in my work
and some of which I cite in this book. See Pineda-Madrid,
Suffering and Salvation.

21. Julia Estela Monárrez Fragoso, *Trama de Una Injusti-
cia: Feminicidio Sexual Sistémico en Ciudad Juárez* (Tijuana, BC,
Mexico: El Colegio de la Frontera Norte, 2009), 9, 105.

22. Diana Washington Valdez, "Mexico on Trial in Murders of Women," *El Paso Times*, April 30, 2009.

23. Chris Arsenault, "In Juárez, Women Just Disappear,"
Al Jazeera, March 8, 2011, https://www.aljazeera.com/
features/2011/3/8/in-juarez-women-just-disappear.

24. Tricia Serviss, "American Rhetorics of Disappearance: Translocal Feminist Problem-Solving Rhetorics,"
in *Crossing Borders, Drawing Boundaries: The Rhetoric of Lines
across America*, ed. Barbara Couture and Patti Wojahn (Boul-
der: University Press of Colorado, 2016), 171–91.

25. "Feminicidio," Observatorio de Igualdad de Género
de América Latina y el Caribe; Linnea Sandin, "Femicides
in Mexico: Impunity and Protests," Center for Strategic &

International Studies, March 19, 2020, https://www.csis
.org/analysis/femicides-mexico-impunity-and-protests.

26. Jorge Ramos, "In Mexico, Women Break the Silence against Femicide," *New York Times*, March 6, 2020, https://www.nytimes.com/2020/03/06/opinion/international-world/mexico-femicides-amlo.html.

27. Victoria Sanford, "From Genocide to Feminicide: Impunity and Human Rights in Twenty-First Century Guatemala," *Journal of Human Rights* 7 (2008).

28. Tamar Diana Wilson, "Introduction: Violence against Women in Latin America," *Latin American Perspectives* 41, no. 1 (January 2014): 9.

29. Deborah Hastings, "In Central America, Women Killed 'with Impunity' Just Because They're Women," *New York Daily News*, January 10, 2014, https://www.nydailynews.com/news/world/femicide-rise-central-america-article-1.1552233. In 2007, Costa Rica became the first Latin American country to pass a law against femicide. See Anastasia Moloney, "Colombia Confronts Femicide, the 'Most Extreme Form of Violence against Women,'" *Reuters,* August 20, 2015, https://www.reuters.com/article/us-colombia-women-murder/colombia-confronts-femicide-the-most-extreme-form-of-violence-against-women-idUSKCN0QP0CM20150820.

30. Angelika Albaladejo, "How Violence Affects Women in El Salvador," Latin American Working Group, February 22, 2016, https://www.lawg.org/how-violence-affects-women-in-el-salvador/.

31. Albaladejo, "How Violence Affects Women in El Salvador."

32. Hastings, "In Central America, Women Killed."

33. Albaladejo, "How Violence Affects Women in El Salvador."

34. Hastings, "In Central America, Women Killed."

35. "Feminicidio," Observatorio de Igualdad de Género de América Latina y el Caribe.

36. Juan Carlos Arita, "Not One More: Ending Femicide in Honduras," *Oxfam Views & Voices*, March 8, 2016, https://views-voices.oxfam.org.uk/2016/03/not-one-more-ending-femicide-in-honduras/.

37. Marina Prieto-Carrón, Marilyn Thomson, and Mandy Macdonald, "No More Killings! Women Respond to Femicides in Central America," *Gender and Development* 15, no. 1 (March 2007): 26. See also M. Kennedy, "The Feminisation of Poverty, and the Impact of Globalisation on Women," paper presented at the School for Policy Studies, University of Bristol, April 11, 2005.

38. Rashida Manjoo, "United Nation's Human Rights Council—Report of Special Rapporteur on Violence against Women, Its Causes and Consequences—on the Killing of Women," in Laurent et al., *Femicide*, 112.

39. Loes Van Der Graaf, "Organized Crime–Related Femicide," in Laurent et al., *Femicide*, 68, https://femicideincanada.ca/sites/default/files/2017-12/ACUNS%20%282014%29%20FEMICIDE%2C%20GLOBAL%20ISSUE%20THAT%20DEMANDS%20ACTION_VOLUME%202.pdf.

40. Manjoo, "United Nations Human Rights Council," 111.

41. Hastings, "In Central America, Women Killed."

42. "Feminicidio," Observatorio de Igualdad de Género de América Latina y el Caribe.

43. Adriaan Alsema, "Femicide in Colombia Left at Least 44 Victims So Far This Year, and One Girl Impaled," *Colombia*

Reports, March 4, 2020, https://colombiareports.com/femi
cide-in-colombia-left-at-least-44-victims-so-far-this-year
-and-one-girl-impaled/.

44. Alsema, "Femicide in Colombia."

45. Bueno-Hansen, "Feminicidio," 290–311.

46. In Defense of the Rights of Women. See DEMUS's
website at http://www.demus.org.pe.

47. Bueno-Hansen, "Feminicidio."

48. "Feminicidio," Observatorio de Igualdad de Género
de América Latina y el Caribe; "Femicide and International
Women's Rights: An Epidemic of Violence in Latin America,"
Global Americans Report, 2020, https://theglobalamericans
.org/reports/femicide-international-womens-rights/.

49. Tamar Diana Wilson, "Introduction: Violence against
Women in Latin America," *Latin American Perspectives* 41, no.
1 (January 2014): 13.

50. "Feminicidio," Observatorio de Igualdad de Género
de América Latina y el Caribe.

51. Agencia de Noticias Fides, "Bolivia es el país de
Sudamérica con más feminicidios, ya suman 21 en este
2020," February 14, 2020, https://www.noticiasfides.com/
nacional/sociedad/bolivia-es-el-pais-de-sudamerica-con
-mas-feminicidios-ya-suman-21-en-este-2020-403574.

52. "Observatorio de femicidios—Informe Final 2020,"
Defensoría del Pueblo de la Nación Argentina, December
31, 2020, http://www.dpn.gob.ar/observatorio-femicidios
.php.

53. Marta Fontenla, "Femicides in Mar del Plata," trans.
Sara Koopman, in Fregoso and Bejarano, *Terrorizing Women*,
116–26. For an extensive account of Argentina's feminicide
victims and the ensuing protests against this tragedy, see

Paula Rodríguez, *#NiUnaMenos* (Buenos Aires, Argentina: Grupo Editorial Planeta, 2015).

54. Andrada Filip, Michael Platzer, et al., *Femicide: Target of Women in Conflict, A Global Issue That Demands Action*, vol. 3 (Vienna, Austria: The Academic Council on the United Nations System [ACUNS], 2015); Simona Demazetoska, Michael Platzer, and Gejsi Plaku, *Femicide: A Global Issue That Demands Action*, vol. 2 (Vienna, Austria: The Academic Council on the United Nations System [ACUNS], 2014).

55. See, e.g., Christine Zuni Cruz et al., *New Mexico Missing and Murdered Indigenous Women and Relatives Task Force Report*, State of New Mexico, Department of Indian Affairs, December 2020, https://www.niwrc.org/resources/report/new-mexico-missing-and-murdered-indigenous-women-and-relatives-task-force-report; Nicole MartinRogers and Virginia Pendleton, *Missing and Murdered Indigenous Women Task Force: A Report to the Minnesota Legislature*, Minnesota Department of Public Safety and Wilder Research, December 2020, https://dps.mn.gov/divisions/ojp/Documents/missing-murdered-indigenous-women-task-force-report.pdf.

56. Thistlethwaite, *Women's Bodies as Battlefield*, 8.

57. For an extended discussion, see Thistlethwaite, *Women's Bodies as Battlefield*, 83–125.

58. Thistlethwaite, *Women's Bodies as Battlefield*, 109, 127.

59. Elisabeth Schüssler Fiorenza, *Rhetoric and Ethic: The Politics of Biblical Studies* (Minneapolis: Fortress Press, 1999), 5.

60. Thistlethwaite, *Women's Bodies as Battlefield*, 3–4.

61. Julia Estela Monárrez Fragoso, "The Victims of the Ciudad Juárez Feminicide: Sexually Fetishized Commodities," in Fregoso and Bejarano, *Terrorizing Women*, 64–65; Marta

Fontenla, "Femicides in Mar del Plata," trans. Sara Koopman, in Fregoso and Bejarano, *Terrorizing Women*, 116–26.

62. Thistlethwaite, *Women's Bodies as Battlefield*, 7.

63. Janet R. Jakobsen, "Gender in the Production of Religious and Secular Violence," in Murphy, *Blackwell Companion to Religion and Violence*, 129.

64. Thistlethwaite, *Women's Bodies as Battlefield*, 4.

65. Thistlethwaite, *Women's Bodies as Battlefield*, 2.

66. Thistlethwaite, *Women's Bodies as Battlefield*, 3.

67. Carlos Mendoza-Álvarez, *La Resurrección Como Anticipación Mesiánica: Duelo, Memoria y Esperanza Desde Los Sobrevivientes* (Mexico City: Universidad Iberoamericana, A.C., 2020), 49. Translation mine.

68. M. Shawn Copeland, *Knowing Christ Crucified: The Witness of African American Religious Experience* (Maryknoll, NY: Orbis Books, 2018), 131.

69. Achille Mbembe, *Necro-Politics* (Durham, NC: Duke University Press, 2019).

70. Copeland, *Knowing Christ Crucified*, 131.

71. Thistlethwaite, *Women's Bodies as Battlefield*, 129.

72. Marcella Althaus-Reid, "Doing a Theology from Disappeared Bodies: Theology, Sexuality, and the Excluded Bodies of the Discourses of Latin American Liberation Theology," in *The Oxford Handbook of Feminist Theology*, ed. Mary McClintock Fulkerson and Sheila Briggs (Oxford: Oxford University Press, 2012), 442.

73. Althaus-Reid, "Doing a Theology from Disappeared Bodies," 443.

74. Juan Carlos Arita, "Not One More."

75. Ignacio Ellacuría, "Discernir 'El Signo' de los Tiempos," in *Escritos Teológicos*, vol. 2/1 (San Salvador, El Salvador: UCA Editores, 2000), 133–35. English translation is

from Kevin F. Burke, "The Crucified People as 'Light for the Nations': A Reflection on Ignacio Ellacuría," in *Rethinking Martyrdom*, ed. Teresa Okure, Jon Sobrino, and Felix Wilfred, in *Concilium* 2003, no. 1 (2003): 124. See also Ignacio Ellacuría, "Discernir el Signo de los Tiempos," *Diakonia* 17 (1981): 59; Michael E. Lee, *Bearing the Weight of Salvation: The Soteriology of Ignacio Ellacuría* (New York: Crossroad Publishing, 2009), 73–104.

76. Althaus-Reid, "Doing a Theology from Disappeared Bodies," 442.

III. SALVATION IN THE
SHADOW OF FEMINICIDE

1. Duncan Forrester, "The Scope of Public Theology," *Studies in Christian Ethics* 17, no. 1 (2004): 6.

2. Roger Haight, *Jesus Symbol of God* (Maryknoll, NY: Orbis, 1999), 335, xii.

3. Haight, *Jesus Symbol of God*, 336.

4. Gustavo Gutiérrez, *A Theology of Liberation* (Maryknoll, NY: Orbis, 1973), 104.

5. Haight, *Jesus Symbol of God*, 335.

6. The phrase *kingdom of God* is not gender inclusive and, along with many feminist theologians, I most often use the word *reign* instead. However, *kingdom of God* denotes a geographic region in which God's will is fully realized. This is the connotation I wish to invoke in this passage; hence my use of the phrase.

7. Haight, *Jesus Symbol of God*, 340.

8. Jon Sobrino, *Jesus the Liberator: A Historical-Theological View* (Maryknoll, NY: Orbis, 1993), 160.

9. Sobrino, *Jesus the Liberator*, 93, 53, 85.

10. Josiah Royce, *Studies of Good and Evil: A Series of Essays upon Problems of Philosophy and of Life* (New York: D. Appleton and Company, 1898), 23.

11. Josiah Royce, *The Sources of Religious Insight* (New York: Charles Scribner's Sons, 1912), 252–55.

12. Haight, *Jesus Symbol of God*, 344–45.

13. Augustine, *Confessions*, X.6; Aquinas, *Summa Theologiae*, I, q.47, a.1.

14. Elizabeth A. Johnson, CSJ, *Creation: Is God's Charity Broad Enough for Bears?* (Los Angeles: Marymount Institute Press, 2014): 9–11.

15. Josiah Royce, *The Problem of Christianity* (Chicago: University of Chicago Press, 1918): 223, 337–42, 362, 374–84.

16. Haight, *Jesus Symbol of God*, 383.

17. Royce, *Sources of Religious Insight*, 266.

18. Royce, *Sources of Religious Insight*, 266–67.

19. Haight, *Jesus Symbol of God*, 387.

20. Haight, *Jesus Symbol of God*, 383, 355–56.

21. Royce, *Studies of Good and Evil*, 23.

22. Haight, *Jesus Symbol of God*, 356.

23. Haight, *Jesus Symbol of God*, 374–75.

24. Haight, *Jesus Symbol of God*, 336.

25. Haight, *Jesus Symbol of God*, 167–68. The quotes within this extended quote are taken from Joseph A. Fitzmyer, *The Gospel according to Luke: Introduction, Translation, and Notes* (Garden City, NY: Doubleday, 1981, 1985), 222; Earl Richard, *Jesus: One and Many; The Christological Concept of New Testament Authors* (Wilmington, DE: Michael Glazier, 1988), 185; and Jerome Neyrey, *The Passion according to Luke: A Redaction Study of Luke's Soteriology* (Mahwah, NJ: Paulist Press, 1985), 184–92.

26. Haight, *Jesus Symbol of God*, 167.

IV. TO BELIEVE IN THE
GOD WHO SAVES

1. Roger Haight, *Jesus Symbol of God* (Maryknoll, NY: Orbis, 1999), 214.

2. Haight, *Jesus Symbol of God*, 215.

3. Walter Brueggemann, *Hope within History* (Atlanta: John Knox Press, 1987).

4. Elisabeth Schüssler Fiorenza, *Rhetoric and Ethic: The Politics of Biblical Studies* (Minneapolis: Fortress Press, 1999), 5.

5. Haight, *Jesus Symbol of God*, 384–85.

6. Carlos Mendoza-Álvarez, *La Resurrección Como Anticipación Mesiánica: Duelo, Memoria y Esperanza Desde Los Sobrevivientes* (Mexico City: Universidad Iberoamericana, A.C., 2020); Achille Mbembe, *Necro-Politics* (Durham, NC: Duke University Press, 2019).

7. Gustavo Gutiérrez, *A Theology of Liberation* (Maryknoll, NY: Orbis, 1973), 152.

8. Gutiérrez, *A Theology of Liberation*, 153.

9. For example, see Nancy Pineda-Madrid, *Suffering and Salvation in Ciudad Juárez* (Minneapolis: Fortress Press, 2011), 97–121; Rosa-Linda Fregoso and Cynthia Bejarano, eds., *Terrorizing Women: Feminicide in the Americas* (Durham, NC: Duke University Press, 2010); Kathleen Staudt and Zulma Y. Mendez, *Courage, Resistance, & Women in Ciudad Juárez: Challenges to Militarization* (Austin: University of Texas Press, 2015); Paula Rodriguez, *#NiUnaMenos* (Ciudad Autónoma de Buenos Aires: Planeta, 2015); Nina Maria Lozano, *Not One More! Feminicidio on the Border* (Columbus: Ohio State University Press, 2019).

10. Elizabeth A. Johnson, "Redeeming the Name of Christ—Christology," in *Freeing Theology: The Essentials of*

Theology in Feminist Perspective (New York: HarperCollins, 1993), 119–20.

11. Haight, *Jesus Symbol of God*, 387–88.

12. Johann Baptist Metz, "On the Way to a Christology after Auschwitz," in *Who Do You Say That I Am? Confessing the Mystery of Christ*, ed. John C. Cavadini and Laura Holt, trans. J. Matthew Ashley (Notre Dame, IN: University of Notre Dame Press, 2004), 147.

13. Pineda-Madrid, *Suffering and Salvation*, 66.

14. Haight, *Jesus Symbol of God*, 366.

15. M. Shawn Copeland, *Knowing Christ Crucified: The Witness of African American Religious Experience* (Maryknoll, NY: Orbis, 2018), 147.

16. J. Matthew Ashley, "Johann Baptist Metz," in *The Blackwell Companion to Political Theology*, ed. Peter Scott and William T. Cavanaugh (Malden, MA: Blackwell Publishing, 2007), 244, 245.

17. Marcella Althaus-Reid, "Doing a Theology from Disappeared Bodies: Theology, Sexuality, and the Excluded Bodies of the Discourses of Latin American Liberation Theology," in *The Oxford Handbook of Feminist Theology*, ed. Sheila Briggs and Mary McClintock Fulkerson (Oxford: Oxford University Press, 2011), 443.

18. Mendoza-Álvarez, *La Resurrección Como Anticipación Mesiánica*, 86.

19. Loes Van Der Graaf, "Organized Crime–Related Femicide," in *Femicide: A Global Issue That Demands Action*, ed. Claire Laurent, Michael Platzer, and Maria Idomir (Vienna: Academic Council on the United Nations System [ACUNS]), 69.

20. Charis McGowan, "'Our Role Is Central': More Than 1m Chilean Women to March in Huge Protest," *The Guard-*

ian, March 6, 2020, https://www.theguardian.com/world/2020/mar/06/chile-womens-day-protest.

21. Pineda-Madrid, *Suffering and Salvation*, 97–121.

22. May Our Daughters Return Home.

23. Jon Sobrino, *Christ the Liberator: A View from the Victims*, trans. Paul Burns (Maryknoll, NY: Orbis, 2001), 48. Italics in the original.

24. Josiah Royce, "The Problem of Job," in *Studies of Good and Evil: A Series of Essays upon Problems of Philosophy and of Life* (New York: D. Appleton and Company, 1898), 23, 24.

25. Copeland, *Knowing Christ Crucified*, 145.

26. Ignacio Ellacuría, "Discernir 'El Signo' de los Tiempos," in *Escritos Teológicos*, vol. 2/1 (San Salvador, El Salvador: UCA Editores, 2000), 133–35. English translation is from Kevin F. Burke, "The Crucified People as 'Light for the Nations': A Reflection on Ignacio Ellacuría," in *Rethinking Martyrdom*, ed. Teresa Okure, Jon Sobrino, and Felix Wilfred, in *Concilium* 2003, no. 1 (2003): 124.

27. As quoted by Kevin F. Burke. See Kevin F. Burke, *The Ground beneath the Cross: The Theology of Ignacio Ellacuría* (Washington, DC: Georgetown University Press, 2000), 181.

28. Ignacio Ellacuría, "Discernir el Signo de los Tiempos," *Diakonia* 17 (1981): 59.

29. Ivone Gebara, *Out of the Depths: Women's Experience of Evil and Salvation* (Minneapolis: Fortress Press, 2002), 116–17.

30. Elizabeth A. Johnson. *She Who Is: The Mystery of God in Feminist Theological Discourse* (New York: Crossroad, 1992), 14.

31. Gebara, *Out of the Depths*, 113.

32. Johnson, "Redeeming the Name of Christ," 119.

33. Johnson, "Redeeming the Name of Christ," 119.

34. This quote is taken from "What Life Means to Einstein: An Interview by George Sylvester Viereck," *The Saturday Evening Post* (October 26, 1929).

35. Roberto S. Goizueta, "Fiesta: Life in the Subjunctive," in *From the Heart of Our People: Latino/a Explorations in Catholic Systematic Theology*, ed. Orlando O. Espín and Miguel H. Díaz (Maryknoll, NY: Orbis, 1999), 84–99.

36. Elisabeth Schüssler Fiorenza, *Jesus: Miriam's Child, Sophia's Prophet; Critical Issues in Feminist Christology* (New York: Continuum, 1994), 123.

37. Schüssler Fiorenza, *Jesus*, 123–24.

38. Schüssler Fiorenza, *Jesus*, 125.

39. Haight, *Jesus Symbol of God*, 348.

40. Robin Ryan, *Jesus and Salvation: Soundings in the Christian Tradition and Contemporary Theology* (Collegeville, MN: Liturgical Press, 2015), 27.

INDEX